CALIFORNIA PICTORIAL

Chronicles of California

CALIFORNIA

PICTORIAL

A History in Contemporary Pictures, 1786 to 1859

With Descriptive Notes on Pictures and Artists

JEANNE VAN NOSTRAND AND EDITH M. COULTER

UNIVERSITY OF CALIFORNIA PRESS

BERKELEY AND LOS ANGELES · 1948

UNIVERSITY OF CALIFORNIA PRESS
BERKELEY, CALIFORNIA

◇

CAMBRIDGE UNIVERSITY PRESS
LONDON, ENGLAND

PRINTED IN THE UNITED STATES OF AMERICA
BY THE UNIVERSITY OF CALIFORNIA PRESS

PREFACE

FROM EARLIEST DAYS, *men, seeking to make a permanent record of their impressions in a medium more vivid than words, have used pencil and brush to supplement written records. When the first books were printed in the early fifteenth century they contained crude woodcut illustrations intended to enliven and embellish the text. The scenes depicted in most of these first woodcuts were products of the artist's imagination, but gradually, as new techniques were discovered, the practice of using engravings based on accurate contemporary sketches became more common. By the eighteenth century books of voyages were appearing with illustrations engraved from drawings made "on-the-spot."*

The pictures made in the course of official governmental explorations were usually the work of artists sent on the voyages especially for the purpose of recording the topography, the flora, the fauna, and the arts of the countries visited. Although the artist's drawings were part of the official records and were presumably deposited with the reports and preserved in governmental archives, many have survived only through the reproductions which were made for the published report. The pictures made by the official artists of the various European exploring expeditions which visited California are not numerous, but they definitely show the British, French, and Russian interests in the future development of the West Coast. A far greater number of pictures made by unofficial visitors to California—adventurers, soldiers, sailors, traders, surveyors, miners, and settlers—show the Mexican period in California's history, the migration brought about by the discovery of gold, and the telescoping of a century of progress into the ten years following the gold discovery. Since these unofficial graphic records of contemporary events were the property of the artists they have remained in private hands, or, after passing from collector to collector, have finally been deposited in public museums, libraries, or galleries.

Except for the artists engaged for the early official explorations, no one was assigned the task of making a pictorial record of California. The choice of the subject to be painted depended on the artist, and he made his selection from the events and people that happened to interest him. From the resulting heterogeneous collection of pictures, a representative selection for the period 1786 to 1859 has been made for this book.

An attempt has been made to use original pictures whenever possible, even though many of them are blackened and discolored with age. Some of the scenes in the pictures are here identified for the first time. A narrative background places each picture in its proper historical setting. The long lapse of time between the early explorations and the resulting lack of eyewitness accounts of California presented some difficulties in preparing a continuous story to accompany Plates I to XXIV. The availability of numerous contemporary accounts made possible a more closely woven account for the period 1849 to 1859.

The emphasis in the first sections is necessarily on Monterey, the port of call for early visitors, and its immediate vicinity. In the later sections the scope widens to include the exploration and settlement brought about by the discovery of gold. Southern California is less well represented than the northern part of the state as its development took place after the gold rush period.

Opposite each plate will be found information concerning the life and work of the artist and descriptive notes on the pictures. This information has been gleaned from many sources, both printed and manuscript—journals, diaries, newspapers, catalogues of art exhibits—and from correspondents with descendants of the artists. Research has been carried on in public and in private collections in California, elsewhere in the United States, and in Europe.

We wish to acknowledge gratefully the help given us by the staffs of the Bancroft Library, California Historical Society Library, Frick Art Reference Library, Society of California Pioneers Library, Huntington Library, M. H. de Young Memorial Museum, the Southwest Museum, the New York Historical Society, Sutter's Fort Historical Museum, and the California State Library.

We also desire to express our appreciation to those who graciously permitted us to reproduce pictures from their private collections. Separate acknowledgments for these favors appear with each plate.

J.V.N.
E.M.C

CONTENTS

CONTENTS

CONTENTS

CALIFORNIA
BEFORE THE GOLD RUSH

Spanish California, 1786-1822

PLATE 1: NOTES

GASPARD DUCHÉ DE VANCY, draughtsman, painter, and engraver, accompanied the La Pérouse expedition as artist. He lost his life when the *Astrolabe* was wrecked.

The painting by De Vancy is believed to be the second recorded view of the mission and the copies of it are the earliest surviving records of an actual California scene. It was apparently left with the mission fathers, for both Malaspina and Beechey, later visitors, describe it. Mrs. James L. Ord, in her manuscript *Occurrencias en California,* says that Father Moreno gave the painting to her brother, Juan de la Guerra, in 1833, and that he in turn gave it to her just before his death, but that it disappeared from among her possessions a few years later. A copy of the painting is now in the Museo Naval, Madrid. Henry Raup Wagner believes that the copy may have been made by Tomás de Suría in 1791, or by José Cordero in 1792.

There is a record of an earlier painting in the inventory of the possessions of Mission San Carlos, dated February 5, 1775, sent by Father Junípero Serra to Viceroy Bucardi in Mexico. The inventory lists two framed oil paintings, each a yard in height, one of San Carlos and another of San Buenaventura. There is no further record of these unless a painting once in the possession of the Society of California Pioneers is the early view of San Carlos. This picture, described as a painting of a scene at the mission by Cristóbal Díaz, chaplain of the ship *San Carlos,* was destroyed in the San Francisco fire of 1906.

Reception of La Pérouse at Carmel Mission. 1786

Artist: GASPARD DUCHÉ DE VANCY

From a photograph of the painting in Museo Naval, *Publicaciones,* No. I.

Resivimiento del Conde delas Pei Rus enla mision del Carmalo de Montenni

PLATE 1

In september, 1786, the French scientific and commercial expedition under the command of Jean François Galaup de la Pérouse entered Monterey Bay—the first visit of foreigners to any of the Spanish establishments in California. Monterey Bay had been discovered and named by Sebastian Vizcaíno in 1602 in his search for safe harbors in which the Manila galleons might anchor and obtain fresh water and food on the long return trip from the Philippines to Acapulco. Vizcaíno urged the King to authorize a settlement there, but it was not until 1770 that a mission and presidio were established at Monterey. In 1775 a royal decree made Monterey the residence of the governor of California, and when the La Pérouse expedition arrived eleven years later it was greeted cordially by the Spanish officials there. The religious at Mission San Carlos Borroméo, the permanent buildings of which were located on Carmel Bay, a few miles from the presidio at Monterey, also welcomed them, and it is this welcome which is portrayed in this sketch by De Vancy, which shows the mission buildings as they looked at that time. After a stay of ten days, the expedition left the harbor, its two ships loaded with fresh food given them by the Spaniards. Less than two years later both ships disappeared in the Pacific.

Plate 2: Notes

Tomás de Suría, believed to be the painter of the "View," came to Mexico in 1778. He joined the Malaspina expedition at Acapulco, taking the place of the artist, Brambila, who was forced by illness to remain in Mexico. Suría returned to Mexico and presumably sent the picture to Spain to be included in the report of the expedition. This report remained in manuscript until 1885, when it was published in Madrid with the title *Viaje politíco-científico abrededor del mundo por las corbetas Descubierta y Atrevida.* The six engravings reproduced from paintings made by the artist of the expedition do not include the "View of the Presidio of Monterey."

View of the Presidio of Monterey. 1791

Artist: Tomás de Suría

From a photograph of the original water color in Museo Naval, *Publicaciones,* No. I.

PLATE 2

THE PRESIDIO at Monterey was established on June 3, 1770, and by 1791, when the Spanish expedition under the command of Alejandro Malaspina anchored in Monterey Bay, it consisted of a group of buildings forming a square. The barracks for the soldiers and the storehouses were built of wood and had mud roofs, the chapel and the governor's house were of adobe construction. Malaspina had sailed from Cadiz in 1789 for a tour of the world and after exploring the coasts of South America, Panama, and Mexico he sailed north as far as Cape Mendocino before visiting Monterey. The first American to land in California, a gunner named John Groem who accompanied the expedition,

died and was buried at Mission San Carlos, which was situated a few miles from the Monterey presidio.

The "View of the Presidio," credited by Henry Raup Wagner to Tomás de Suría, the artist of the Malaspina expedition, is believed to be the earliest picture of the military installation at the capital. The painting is unsigned and there is a possibility, states Wagner, that it was the work of José Cordero, an artist who accompanied the Galiano–Valdés expedition in 1792. The view is sketched from the slope at the rear of the presidio and looks toward the bay, where two vessels are anchored, perhaps the *Atrevida* and the *Descubierta* of the Malaspina expedition.

PLATE 3: NOTES

JOHN SYKES was born in England in 1773. He entered the navy at an early age and was rapidly promoted. He commanded the *Adamant* in the attack upon Flushing in 1809, became a rear admiral in 1838 and shortly before his death in 1858 was promoted to an admiralship. Sykes accompanied the Vancouver expedition as artist. The sketches made by him were deposited with Vancouver's official report and are in the possession of the Hydrographic Office of the Admiralty, London. Three views of California scenes drawn by him appear in the published report of Vancouver's voyage: *Voyage of Discovery to the North Pacific Ocean,* 1798. The engravings by William Alexander, made from Sykes' drawings for the report, are in the Ayer Collection of the Newberry Library, Chicago.

For additional notes on the artist, see plate 4.

Presidio of Monterey. 1794

Artist: JOHN SYKES

From an engraving in Vancouver's *Voyage of Discovery to the North Pacific Ocean,* 1798.

PLATE 3

CAPTAIN GEORGE VANCOUVER, who commanded three vessels sent out by the English admiralty in 1791, was the second foreign visitor to California. He had been instructed to explore the North Pacific, and to see that the provisions of the Nootka Convention were carried out. After meeting the Spanish commissioner at Nootka, he sailed down the coast and on November 14, 1792, entered San Francisco Bay in the *Discovery*. He was received by Comandante Sal at the presidio and by the padres at the mission. The British party was taken to visit Santa Clara Mission by the Spanish officials—the first time that foreigners had journeyed into the interior of California. Re-turning to San Francisco, Vancouver went to Monterey, where he was received cordially.

On his second visit to California, in the following year, Vancouver was surprised to find that the attitude of the acting governor, José Joaquín Arrillaga, was no longer friendly. Arrillaga objected to the opportunity which had been given the visitors, on their first visit, to observe the weakness of the Spanish military installations, and placed many restrictions on them. It is likely, therefore, that this view of the presidio at Monterey was sketched by John Sykes, the artist who accompanied the expedition, on either the first visit or on the third, in 1794, which was uneventful. The view was sketched from Fort Hill.

THE WATER COLOR of the Carmel mission by John Sykes from which this engraving was made is the third known view of the mission. It shows not only the first crude buildings, the huts for the Indians, and the foundations of the new church but also the activities of the mission community. The original sketch is labeled The "Mission of St. Carlos near Monterey," and measures eight by fifteen inches. It is in the possession of the Hydrographic Office of the Admiralty, London. The engraver of the plate for the published report adhered faithfully to the Sykes drawing.

For additional notes on the artist, see plate 3.

Mission of San Carlos. 1794

Artist: JOHN SYKES

From an engraving in Vancouver's *Voyage of Discovery to the North Pacific Ocean,* 1798.

PLATE 4

SHORTLY AFTER the establishment of the mission at San Diego and the arrival of the relief ship *San Antonio* with supplies from Mexico, the founding of a second mission was undertaken. Father Serra, on the *San Antonio,* and Governor Portolá, by land, started north to find a location for a mission on the Bay of Monterey. Portolá reached the bay, the *San Antonio* arrived, and on June 3, 1770, the Mission San Carlos Borroméo de Monterey was founded and the Presidio of Monterey established. A year later the mission was moved to a site near the mouth of the Carmel River, on a rise overlooking Carmel Bay.

The rude architecture of the early mission buildings was fairly uniform. A rectangular space was marked off and the wooden and grass-roofed buildings were constructed within the square. At Carmel four buildings—a church, a house for the Fathers, a storehouse, and a guard-house—were erected within a forty by seventy yard space.

Construction was started on the new church (the present) in July, 1793. The sketch of the mission by John Sykes shows the rough buildings and the foundations of the new church. It was therefore probably made on the occasion of Vancouver's third visit to Monterey, in 1794.

WILHELM GOTTLIEF TILESIUS VON TILENAU, artist and naturalist, was born at Mühlhausen in 1769 and died in 1857. He accompanied the Krusenstern expedition and made the sketches for Langsdorff's *Bemerkungen auf einer Reise um die Welt*. These are unsigned but Langsdorff writes "thanks are due to my friend and travelling companion Councillor Tilesius, who unites to the most extensive scientific knowledge exquisite taste in the fine arts, for the many sketches with which he has already favored me and for the many more promised by him to enrich and embellish . . . my travels."

For additional notes on the artist, see plate 6.

View of the Spanish Establishments at San Francisco. 1806

Artist: WILHELM GOTTLIEF TILESIUS VON TILENAU

From an engraving in Langsdorff, *Bemerkungen auf einer Reise um die Welt,* 1812.

PLATE 5

THE PRESIDIO of San Francisco was founded in 1776, and by 1806 nineteen missions, four presidios, and three pueblos had been established, giving Spain a tenuous control of the coast of California from San Diego Bay to San Francisco Bay. In 1784 a small company of Russians settled at Kodiak, later moving to Sitka, but found it difficult to obtain sufficient food to maintain a colony throughout the winter. In 1803 Czar Alexander I sent out a Russian expedition under the command of Admiral Krusenstern to inspect the Russian colonies in the North Pacific. Georg Heinrich Langsdorff and

Nikolai Rezánof, members of the party, left the main expedition, visited the Aleutian Islands, and in 1806, in search of supplies for the Russian settlements, entered San Francisco Bay in the *Juno*. Rezánof secured food and arranged for further trade with California.

On Langsdorff's return to St. Petersburg he prepared for publication his *Bemerkungen auf einer Reise um die Welt*, which appeared in 1812. Two California scenes were among the illustrations. The "View of the Spanish Establishments at San Francisco" shows the buildings of the presidio as seen from the Golden Gate.

PLATE 6: NOTES

IN HIS *Bemerkungen auf einer Reise um die Welt* Langsdorff gives a detailed description of the habits and ceremonies of the Indians, and describes at some length the dance arranged for his entertainment at the mission. He writes: "In their dances they remain always in the same place, endeavouring partly with their bows and arrows, partly with their feathers they hold in their hands and wear upon their heads, partly by measured springs, by different movements of their bodies and by the variations of their countenances to represent battles or scenes of domestic life. Their music consists of singing and clapping with a stick, which is split at the end. Their heads, ears and necks were set off with a great variety of ornaments but the bodies, except for a covering about the waist, were naked."

For additional notes on the artist, see plate 5.

Dance of the Indians at the Mission of San Jose. 1806

Artist: WILHELM GOTTLIEF TILESIUS VON TILENAU

From an engraving in Langsdorff, *Bemerkungen auf einer Reise um die Welt*, 1812.

14

PLATE 6

Father firmin lasuén, President of the Missions, had urged the establishment of additional missions, farther inland, with the hope of bringing all the Indians of the coast between San Diego and San Francisco under the control of the Church. Exploration of suitable sites was undertaken in 1795, and authorization for the establishment of five new missions was given by the viceroy the following year. A party left Monterey for the north and traveled as far as the present site of Oakland, but turning back, decided on a location to the south for Mission San José de Guadalupe. The mission was founded by Father Lasuén in June, 1797, and prospered. Georg Heinrich Langsdorff, surgeon and naturalist, accompanied Rezánof on the *Juno* in 1806. In the course of his stay at San Francisco Bay he visited the San José mission and was probably the first representative of a foreign country to explore the southern reaches of the bay. Langsdorff showed great interest in the Indians and their customs. When he reached San José de Guadalupe he was cordially received and a promise made to him in San Francisco was kept, namely, that if he would visit the mission, a dance of the Indians would be arranged.

PLATE 7: NOTES

LOUIS CHORIS, Russian painter, was born in 1795. He received his first art training in Moscow and was appointed to accompany the naturalist F. A. Marschall von Bieberstein on an expedition to the Caucasus. The excellence of Choris' drawings of botanical specimens which Bieberstein collected led to his selection as the official draughtsman of the Otto von Kotzebue expedition. When the voyage was concluded, Choris went to Paris where he prepared for publication his *Voyage pittoresque autour du monde*. The drawing of the presidio which he had made was considerably embellished by the engraver for inclusion in this volume. In 1826 he published a second work, *Vues et paysages des régions equinoxialles, recueillies dans un voyage autour du monde*. On a later visit to America he was killed near Vera Cruz, Mexico.

For additional notes on the artist, see plate 8.

View of the Presidio, San Francisco. 1816

Artist: LOUIS CHORIS

From the original painting. Courtesy of Roger D. Lapham, San Francisco.

PLATE 7

AFTER THE DEPARTURE of Rezánof, California was visited by other Russian officials. In 1809 Baránof, the governor of Alaska, sent Kuskof to trade and to search for suitable sites for settlement. He anchored in Bodega Bay and explored the neighboring country. As a result of his survey, a colony of one hundred Russians and an equal number of Aleuts was settled near the mouth of the present Russian River. A fort, later known as Fort Ross, was constructed.

In 1815 Russia sent an expedition to explore the South Pacific under Captain Otto von Kotzebue. Members of the party included Dr. Ivan Eschscholtz, surgeon; Adelbert von Chamisso and Martin Wormskhold, naturalists; and Louis Choris, artist. The *Rurik*, flying the flag of the Russian navy, entered the Bay of San Francisco in October, 1816. The officers were entertained at Mission Dolores and at the presidio.

The Presidio of San Francisco had been established in 1776. The Spanish government failed, as did the Mexicans later, to support the presidios adequately, and there were comparatively few soldiers stationed at them. In 1835 the last troops were removed from San Francisco to Sonoma and the buildings of the presidio fell into ruins. Luis Argüello was acting as *comandante* at the time of Kotzebue's visit in 1816. The Russians were cordially received and Louis Choris made a water-color sketch of the presidio.

Plate 8: Notes

Choris' *Voyage pittoresque autour du monde* contained four plates of scenes in California: "View of the Presidio of San Francisco in 1816," "A Game of the Natives of California," "Boat of the Port of San Francisco," "Dance of the Inhabitants of California at the Mission of San Francisco, 1816," and several plates showing headdress, weapons, and utensils of the natives. The originals were held in private hands until offered for sale in 1939. With the exception of the "View of the Presidio of San Francisco" they are now in the possession of Donald Angus of Honolulu.

For additional notes on the artist, see plate 7.

Dance of the Inhabitants of California at the Mission of San Francisco. 1816

Artist: Louis Choris

From the original painting. Courtesy of Donald Angus, Honolulu.

PLATE 8

THE MISSION of San Francisco de Asís, better known as the Mission Dolores, was founded in 1776 by Fathers Palou and Cambon. They had come from Monterey in June with Lieutenant José Moraga and a party of soldiers for the purpose of establishing a presidio and a mission at San Francisco Bay. The padres had camped on the Laguna de los Dolores while waiting for the arrival of the *San Carlos* with supplies and built the mission there; hence its familiar name. The dedication of this, the sixth of the California missions, took place on October 9, 1776. The new church was started in 1782 and dedicated in 1791. At no time was there a large Indian population and with the establishment of San Rafael Arcángel, across the bay, in 1817, the number declined. The Mission Dolores was among the first of the Franciscan missions to be secularized and for a period of twenty years was little used. In 1858, however, it was returned to the jurisdiction of the Catholic Church.

In 1816, the year of the visit of the Russian explorers, all of the buildings had been completed and the activities of the mission were at their height. The Indians continued to perform their ceremonial dances, most of which had a religious origin, even after they had ostensibly been converted to Christianity. They were permitted to do so by the Franciscan fathers who, either failing to understand the significance of the dances or remaining tactfully blind to it, considered them a form of amusement.

19

Mexican California, 1823-1846

THE ARTIST, William Smyth, as was the fashion in the early nineteenth century, included a sketch of himself in the act of drawing the picture of Monterey. Attended by two sailors from the *Blossom,* he is seen seated on the hillside at the right of the sketch. From this elevation he depicts the Royal Presidio Church, the homes of the residents, a few by this date being Americans, the lagoon (Washerwomen's Bay) with the Gabilan Mountains in the distance. The original is signed W. Smyth, 1827, and is a faithful representation of the pueblo as it was shortly after California had passed from Spanish to Mexican control.

For additional notes on the artist, see plates 10 and 11.

Presidio and Pueblo of Monterey. 1827

Artist: WILLIAM SMYTH

From the original water color in the collection of Edith M. Coulter, Berkeley.

PLATE 9

IN 1823 MEXICO threw off the last political ties which bound it to Spain, and California became a Mexican province. England and France continued to show interest in the Pacific, as evidenced by the visits of Beechey, Belcher, Simpson, Petit-Thouars, Bernard du Hautcilly, Laplace, and Duflot de Mofras. There were even rumors of the annexation of California by England. In 1825 the English admiralty placed Captain Frederick Beechey in command of an expedition to the Arctic in the sloop of war *Blossom.* The object of the voyage was to explore Bering Strait from the west, and to attempt to meet two other exploring parties, one under the command of Captain Parry, the other under Captain Franklin, which were exploring the strait from the east. Beechey was instructed to remain in Arctic waters during the summer and to winter in a southern latitude. Accordingly, visits were made to San Francisco and Monterey bays in the winters of 1826 and 1827. In the published report of *A Narrative of a Voyage to the Pacific and Beerings Strait,* Beechey gives an interesting account of his sojourn, together with observations made by three of his officers on an overland journey from Yerba Buena to Monterey. Visits were made to the missions, the naturalist collected plants, birds, and marine life, and the artist of the expedition sketched the missions and the presidios. The view of the "Presidio and Pueblo of Monterey" is the earliest known view of the scattered buildings of the capital.

WILLIAM SMYTH, a British naval officer and one of the artists of the Beechey expedition, painted at least eight scenes in California. Only one view, "Californians Throwing the Lasso," was included in Beechey's *Narrative*. The other sketches appeared for the first time in Alexander Forbes' *California: A History of Upper and Lower California,* London, 1839. William Smyth later served as the artist of Sir George Back's expedition in H.M.S. *Terror.* In 1836 there was published in London the *Narrative of a Journey from Lima to Para,* which also contained illustrations from sketches made by him. William Smyth reached the rank of rear admiral in the British navy. He died on September 25, 1877, at Tunbridge Wells.

For additional notes on the artist, see plates 9 and 11.

The Mission of San Carlos, Upper California. 1827

Artist: WILLIAM SMYTH

From the original water color in the David I. Bushnell Collection, Peabody Museum, Harvard University.

PLATE 10

ISSION SAN CARLOS BORROMÉO, which was founded at Monterey on June 3, 1770, by Father Junípero Serra, was moved in December, 1771, to a site in the fertile valley of the Carmel River. The mission was the home of Father Serra during the remainder of his life and after his death continued to be the permanent headquarters of the Father-presidents of all the missions in California. Beneath the sanctuary are buried Fathers Serra, Lasuén, Crespi, and Lópes.

The plan of secularizing the missions which began under Governor Echeandéa in 1831 was carried out under the administration of Governor Figueroa, and by 1834 the friars of sixteen missions in California had been dispossessed, Father José Suárez del Real of San Carlos among the number.

The water color by William Smyth shows the new church, dedicated in 1797, the extent of the mission buildings, including the home of the padres, the workshops, and the red-tiled adobe huts of the Indians. Sketched in 1827, it is probably the best recorded picture of the completed buildings before any had fallen into disuse and ruin and indicates the growth which had taken place since 1794, the date of the John Sykes drawing (plate 4).

PLATE 11: NOTES

THE PAINTINGS of William Smyth were apparently kept by him and not deposited with the Beechey report. The location of the original water color of the "Mission of San Francisco" is unknown, although a search has been made for it. The originals of three of his paintings were sold by the Museum Book Store, London, in 1931. The view of the "Carmel Mission" was acquired by David I. Bushnell, Jr., of Washington, D.C., and at his death was given to the Peabody Museum, Harvard University. The "Presidio and Pueblo of Monterey" and the "Bay of Monterey" are in the possession of Edith M. Coulter, Berkeley, California. The similarities of style and composition found in these originals and the lithograph reproduced here indicate that the lithographer made a faithful facsimilie of the original painting.

For additional notes on the artist, see plates 9 and 10.

The Mission of San Francisco, Upper California. 1826 or 1827

Artist: WILLIAM SMYTH

From a lithograph in Alexander Forbes' *California: A History of Upper and Lower California*, 1839.

PLATE 11

THE *Blossom*, under command of Captain Beechey, entered the Bay of San Francisco on November 6, 1826, and remained there until December 29. Beechey was cordially received by the acting *comandante* of the presidio, Ignacio Martínez. He was given permission to make a survey of the bay on condition that he leave a copy of his map with Martínez for his government. Certain hazards to navigation appeared for the first time on Beechey's maps; a dangerous rock four and one half feet below the surface of the water between Alcatraz and Yerba Buena islands was given the name Blossom Rock by the cartographer.

Visits were made to the presidio and to the Mission of San Francisco de Asís. Beechey states that "earlier the mission contained a thousand converts who were housed in small huts around the mission; but at present only 260 remain, some having been sent, it is true, to the new Mission of San Francisco Solano, but sickness and death have dealt with an unsparing hand among the others." The mission lands, although they covered an area of fifteen square miles, were not productive. Food had to be secured from neighboring missions.

The view of the mission by William Smyth shows the church, the mission buildings, and the huts of the Indians, with the Peninsula hills in the background.

PLATE 12: NOTES

AUGUSTE BERNARD DU HAUTCILLY had command of the French ship *Le Héros* which was sent out from Havre by the firm of Lafitte and Company. Bernard du Hautcilly had a good education and was a close observer and an interesting writer. He was accompanied on the voyage by Dr. Paolo Emilio Botta, an Italian archaelogist. In 1834 Du Hautcilly's *Voyage autour du monde* was published in Paris. It contained three illustrations of scenes in California—"View of Monterey," "View of the Mission of San Luis Rey," and "View of the Russian Establishment at Bodega." An edition of the *Voyage* in Italian translated by Dr. Botta was published at Turin, 1841.

View of the Russian Establishment at Bodega (Fort Ross). 1828

   Artist: AUGUSTE BERNARD DU HAUTCILLY

From an engraving in Bernard du Hautcilly's *Voyage autour du monde*. Paris, 1834–1835.

PLATE 12

FRANCE'S interest in California during the Mexican regime is evidenced by the visits of four separate French expeditions. In 1827 Bernard du Hautcilly, in command of the *Héros*, visited the coast of California. His expedition had been sent out by a group of French businessmen who were interested in establishing trade with the Hawaiian Islands and California. Calls were made at the ports of San Francisco, Santa Cruz, Monterey, Santa Barbara, and San Pedro, and in 1828 Fort Ross was visited.

By 1828 the settlement known as Fort Ross, made by the Russians eighteen miles north of Bodega Bay, gave promise of being permanent. The fort was surrounded by a stockade and cannon were mounted to give protection to the buildings within the enclosure. A church, warehouses, headquarters for the officers, and cabins had been constructed. Small huts for the Aleuts, who served as hunters and laborers, were built outside the stockade.

Agriculture and stock raising were not especially successful and the settlement was unable to send much produce to the Russian colonies in Alaska. There was a continued demand from the Mexican authorities that Russia withdraw from California. After twenty-nine years of occupation the property at Fort Ross was sold to John A. Sutter of New Helvetia and the Russians retired from competition with the Californians.

Bernard du Hautcilly's account of his voyage contains a detailed description of the fort, and a sketch—the best of the early illustrations.

Plate 13: Notes

Jean Jacques Vioget was born in Switzerland in 1799. At the age of fifteen he joined Napoleon's army and was later apprenticed to a French naval engineer. Sailing his own boat, the *Delmira,* Vioget reached San Francisco Bay in 1837 and secured the right to trade from the Mexican *comandante.* He made a survey of Yerba Buena in 1839 and was engaged by Sutter to make maps of New Helvetia. For a time Vioget kept a hotel in Yerba Buena and in 1843 he moved to a grant of land near San Jose, where he died in 1855.

The original painting is in the collection of Harry C. Peterson and is on loan to the Wells Fargo Bank Museum, San Francisco.

Yerba Buena (Now San Francisco) in the Spring of 1837

Artist: Jean Jacques Vioget

From the original water color in the Wells Fargo Bank Museum, San Francisco. Courtesy of Austin Peterson.

PLATE 13

Yerba buena, the settlement which later became San Francisco, was built near the most convenient anchorage for vessels visiting the bay. Under Mexican rule restrictions which had been placed on trade by the Spaniards were loosened, and vessels often came in for water, and to obtain supplies from the mission. In 1835, William A. Richardson, a mate on the whaler *Orion*, left his vessel and remained in California. He made trading trips up and down the coast and in 1835 put up a temporary building, the first structure in Yerba Buena, which was replaced a year or two later by an adobe house. General Vallejo appointed him captain of the port, a position he held for some years. Jacob P. Leese, a native of Ohio, had engaged in the Santa Fe trade before coming to California. In 1836 Leese built the second house, near that of Richardson. The following year he obtained permission from Governor Alvarado to erect a storehouse on the beach near the present junction of Montgomery and Commercial streets.

Jean Jacques Vioget in his ship the *Delmira* reached the Bay of San Francisco in 1837 and secured from the Mexican government the right to trade and barter for hides. His impression of the bay is perpetuated in his "Yerba Buena." The water color shows the two houses, those of Richardson and Leese, mentioned above. For some years the sketch hung in the cabin of Vioget's boat. Lithographs were made from the painting by Britton and Rey in 1867.

CYRILLE PIERRE THÉODORE LAPLACE was born in 1793 and died in 1875. He entered the French navy as a young man and advanced rapidly in rank. The government selected him to command two successive, important, scientific expeditions which he directed with credit. On his return from the second voyage in 1841 he was promoted to a rear admiralship and he was later made vice-admiral of the French fleet. The reports of the two expeditions were published, the first—*Voyage autour du monde par les Mers de l'Inde et de la Chine*, 1833–1839, 5 vols.; the second—*Campagne de circumnavigation de la frégate l'Artémise*, 1841–1844, 3 vols.

Carmel Mission. 1839

Artist: CYRILLE LAPLACE

From the engraving in Laplace's *Campagne de circumnavigation de la frégate l'Artémise pendant les années 1837, 1838, 1839, et 1840, 1841.*

PLATE 14

THE MISSIONS had reached the height of their prosperity and influence by 1830. Agitation for their removal from the control of the Franciscan missionaries, which had started earlier, in the Spanish period, became stronger under Mexican rule. In 1833 the Mexican government issued a decree that called for secularization of the twenty-one missions in California. At most missions the padres remained for a time to protect the churches but the Indians scattered, and the buildings fell into ruin. By 1839, an agent appointed by Governor Alvarado to visit each mission and make an inventory found that nine were almost completely destroyed and that most of the others were in a dilapidated condition.

Captain Cyrille Pierre Théodore Laplace, sailing from France in the *Artémise* and reaching the coast of California in 1839, visited San Carlos Mission. An engraving which gives a picture of the mission after ruin and decay had set in appears in the narrative of his voyage. The view, which was made from a spot near the present corner of Santa Lucia and Francisco streets, Carmel, shows the rear of the mission and the mountains beyond the Carmel River.

PLATE 15: NOTES

ALTHOUGH the presence of the American flag in this picture indicates that it was painted some time after July 9, 1846, it is the earliest known picture showing the extent of the buildings at Sonoma during the Mexican period, before any had fallen into disuse or had been destroyed. The name of the artist is unknown.

The sketch was formerly in the possession of Dr. Charles E. von Geldern of Sacramento, by whom it was presented to the California Historical Society. It had earlier belonged to Dr. Von Geldern's granduncle, Charles von Geldern, who came to Sonoma in 1848 and practiced medicine there for many years, and is believed to have been the model for the mounted figure in the foreground.

The view shows the buildings grouped around the plaza, which was used as a parade ground for troops. At the east end of the block are the two-storied adobe barracks with a balcony extending along the front on the second floor. The home of General Vallejo, an L-shaped building, stands just west of the barracks. At the western corner, forming the intersection of the two wings, rises a tower four stories in height. Still further to the west is seen the home of Salvador Vallejo. On the western side of the plaza are the homes of Jacob P. Leese, Victor Prudon and Captain Henry D. Fitch. The mission church is seen beyond the plaza to the east.

Sonoma

Artist: Unknown

From the original water color. Courtesy of the California Historical Society, San Francisco.

PLATE 15

THE MISSION of San Francisco Solano, named for Saint Francis Solano, a Franciscan friar, was founded by Father José Altemira on July 4, 1823, the most northerly of the missions and the last to be established. Although advantageously located in a fertile valley, the mission failed to attain prosperity during its short history, from 1823 to 1834, the year in which it was secularized.

In 1835 Governor Figueroa ordered General Vallejo to establish a garrison and town on the northern frontier as a protection from the Indians and any aggression from the Russian colony at Fort Ross. Vallejo selected a site near the mission for the town, which he named Sonoma. A company of soldiers was transferred from the presidio at San Francisco, and they, with members of the Híjar–Padrés colony from Mexico, formed the community. Gradually Americans settled in the valley, and on June 14, 1846, a small company of thirty-three Americans led by William Ide and Ezekiel Merritt took possession of Sonoma. Lowering the Mexican flag and raising their standard—the Bear flag—they proclaimed the California Republic. General Mariano Vallejo, Captain Salvador Vallejo, and Victor Prudon, a Frenchman who served as General Vallejo's secretary, were taken to Sutter's Fort and held as prisoners for a short time. The declaration of war between the United States and Mexico terminated the movement for an independent California, but the Bear flag of the California Republic survives as the official flag of the State of California.

PLATE 16: NOTES

ALFRED ROBINSON, a native of Massachusetts, came to California in 1829 as a clerk in the *Brookline* and remained as agent for Bryant and Sturgis, merchants of Boston, traveling up and down the coast from San Diego to San Francisco to arrange for the purchase of hides and for the sale of manufactured goods. He remained in California until 1837, when he returned to the East with his wife Anna María, daughter of Don José de la Guerra y Noriega, of Santa Barbara. Robinson was again in California from 1840 to 1842, again as agent for Bryant and Sturgis. In 1846 his book *Life in California* was published anonymously in New York. The book contains seven lithographs made from sketches by Robinson. He returned to California in 1849 to represent the Pacific Mail Steamship Company in San Francisco.

The Presidio or Town of Santa Barbara. 1840

Artist: ALFRED ROBINSON

From a lithograph in Robinson's *Life in California,* 1846.

PLATE 16

AFTER THE Mexican Republic was created in 1823, and the Spanish rule in California replaced by Mexican, restraints which the Spaniards had placed on trade with foreigners were relaxed. American firms were among the first to take advantage of this new business opportunity, and many American ships made the California coastal cities regular ports of call; Santa Barbara was one of these ports.

The Presidio of Santa Barbara, the last of the four established under Spanish rule, was founded in 1782. The name, Santa Barbara, had been given to the channel by Sebastian Vizcaíno, who had entered it one hundred and eighty years before on the feast day of Saint Barbara. Around the presidio were grouped the homes of the Spanish residents, the largest being that of Don José de la Guerra y Noriega. Visitors to Santa Barbara wrote of its beautiful situation, its well-constructed presidio, its red-tiled roofs, and its gracious social life. The Mission of Santa Barbara, situated on high ground northwest of the presidio, was dedicated in 1786 by Father Lasuén. The building shown in this picture, which still stands today, was erected in 1820, replacing three earlier temporary structures. At this mission, the last to pass into private hands, was buried José Figueroa, the Mexican governor under whom the secularization of the missions was carried out.

Plate 17: Notes

THIS VIEW of Mission San Luis Rey appears as plate 23 of the Atlas accompanying Duflot de Mofras's *Exploration du Territoire de l'Oregon, des Californies, et de la Mer Vermeille,* which contains five views of scenes in California. It is apparent that the sketches were not the work of Duflot de Mofras but had been embellished by the engraver from illustrations which had previously appeared, principally from sketches made by William Smyth in 1827 which had been used to illustrate Forbes' *California: A History of Upper and Lower California,* published in London in 1829 (see plates 9, 10, 11). The engraving reproduced here, however, does not resemble Smyth's work, nor has it been found in any other published report. Even so, it was evidently made some years before Duflot de Mofras's visit, as it shows the mission in a state of repair which was not maintained after its secularization.

View of the Mission of San Luis Rey. 1841

Artist: Unknown

From an engraving in Duflot de Mofras's *Exploration du Territoire de l'Oregon, des Californies, et de la Mer Vermeille,* 1844.

38

PLATE 17

EUGÈNE DUFLOT DE MOFRAS was sent, in 1840, by the French minister of foreign affairs on a special mission to visit Mexico and the provinces to the north. He visited Monterey, Sonoma, Fort Ross, and Sutter's Fort. On his return trip to Mazatlán in 1841 he stopped at Santa Barbara, San Luis Rey, and San Diego. Mission San Luis Rey de Francia was founded by Father Lasuén on June 13, 1798, part way between Mission San Diego and San Juan Capistrano, and almost immediately became one of the largest and most prosperous of the missions. Many Indians were attached to its lands.

In 1810 the mission fathers laid the foundations of a new church building, which when completed was considered, next to San Juan Capistrano, the finest mission church in California. San Luis Rey suffered the decline and ruin common to all of the missions after the secularization decree of 1833. During and after the Mexican War, American troops were stationed there. The troops were withdrawn when California became a state and the mission lands were acquired by Americans. In 1855 the Catholic Church regained ownership of the building and a few acres of the land surrounding it; in 1892 the Franciscan Order established a monastery and seminary there and began a program of restoration.

PLATE 18: NOTES

THE NAME of the artist of the water color from which this lithograph was made is unknown, although it is evident that the painting was made on the spot on the occasion of the seizure of Monterey by Commodore Jones, either as a gift for Thomas Larkin, the American consul, or at his request. This has led to the supposition that the sketch was the work of an officer or sailor with the squadron. William H. Meyer, a gunner on the *Cyane*, kept an illustrated journal of the cruise in which he states that he made sketches for residents of Monterey, but Larkin's name is not mentioned. The location of the original water color, if extant, is likewise unknown.

Harbour and City of Monterey. 1842

Artist: Unknown

From a lithograph published in 1851, drawn on stone by Gildermeister.

PLATE 18

IN 1842 DIPLOMATIC relations between the United States and Mexico were strained as a result of United States recognition of the Texas Republic and negotiations for its annexation, and war was regarded as probable. Commodore Thomas ap Catesby Jones was in command of the Pacific squadron of the United States Navy, which consisted of five vessels—the *United States,* the *Cyane,* the *Yorktown,* the *Dale,* and the *Shark.* While at Callao, Peru, he received a report that war between the United States and Mexico had broken out, and that Mexico intended to cede California to Great Britain in order to prevent its seizure by the United States. Hearing further that three British warships then in the Pacific were apparently headed for the California coast, Commodore Jones immediately set sail for Monterey. He entered the bay on October 19, 1842, and on Oc-

tober 20 a detachment of men was landed and the American flag was raised over the Mexican fort. Investigation of Mexican dispatches convinced him that a state of war did not exist, and on October 21 the Mexican flag was restored and the American soldiers withdrawn.

Two water colors, one of the city of Monterey and the other of the harbor and bay, which were later made into lithographs, were painted at this time by an unknown artist. This, the view of the harbor and bay, was sketched from the slope above the town, looking toward the bay and the American vessels at anchor. The large two-story house on the left was the residence of Thomas Larkin, the American consul; the Mexican customhouse is on the right. The homes of the Mexican officials, with their walled gardens, are shown in the center; the Mexican flag flies over the fort.

PLATE 19: NOTES

THE VIEW of the "City of Monterey, 1842" was obviously made by the same artist and on the same occasion as the "Harbour and City of Monterey, 1842" (plate 18). It is evident from Larkin's correspondence that he intended to have lithographs made, and on June 3, 1843, he sent, via Honolulu, the originals to his cousin, the Reverend William Matticks Rogers of Boston. However, it was not until Larkin was in New York in 1851 that the lithographs were produced. Both views were issued in two forms—mounted on rollers or folded in cases. Keys to accompany the lithographs were printed. They indicate, by number, the buildings shown in the views and serve as a directory of residents of Monterey at that date.

City of Monterey. 1842

Artist: Unknown

From a lithograph published in 1851, drawn on stone by Gildermeister. Courtesy of Frances M. Molera, San Francisco.

PLATE 19

ONTEREY, the capital of Alta California under Spain and Mexico, was the place of residence of the governor and of the consuls of foreign countries. By 1840, the presidio buildings had almost disappeared, but a fort on the hill was garrisoned with a few soldiers and armed with twelve or thirteen guns. Thomas O. Larkin was appointed United States consul in 1842. The consulate was one of the finest buildings in Monterey. Americans were welcome in the capital; several had received grants of land in the neighboring area; others were engaged in the commerce of the port. There was, therefore, little surprise and less resistance when the United States squadron entered the bay on October 19, 1842. After the seizure of the fort on October 20, and its restoration to the Californians on the following day, courtesies were exchanged, and a ball was given in honor of the American officers.

A formal apology was made to the Mexican government by Daniel Webster, United States secretary of state, and reparations were promised. Mexico asked that Commodore Jones be tried for his violation of international law, but he was exonerated from all blame by the Secretary of the Navy, and was never brought to trial.

The view of the "City of Monterey, 1842" shows the homes and public buildings in the capital; the customhouse, near the landing place; the *cuartel*, the long building with the flagpole; and the presidio church. The numbered key that accompanied the view gave the names of fifty residents and the location of their homes. Several of the number who were listed were American citizens.

California in Transition, 1846-1848

PLATE 20: NOTES

JOHN MIX STANLEY was born in Canandaigua, New York. He began his career as an artist in Detroit, and in 1842 he traveled in the Southwest, painting pictures of the Indians. He joined the Emory party as artist, and although the view of San Diego is unsigned, it was probably his work. He traveled in Oregon and again visited the Southwest, where he painted one hundred and fifty canvases of the American Indian. The majority of these were destroyed in a fire at the Smithsonian Institute in 1868. Stanley also served as artist with the Pacific Railroad Surveys, conducted by the United States government in the years 1853–1857.

San Diego. 1846

Artist: JOHN MIX STANLEY (?)

From a lithograph in Emory's *Reconnaissance of a Route from Fort Leavenworth to San Diego,* 1849.

PLATE 20

THE SAN DIEGO presidio was established in 1769, when the four expeditions sent from Mexico to colonize California met at the Bay of San Diego. Mission San Diego de Alcalá was founded by Father Junípero Serra in July of the same year. In 1774 the mission was moved six miles inland; the small settlement, later known as Old Town, remained in the original location near the bay.

At the beginning of the Mexican War Lieutenant Colonel William H. Emory, of the U. S. Corps of Topographical Engineers, was sent with a party to reconnoiter a route for General Stephen W. Kearny, whose troops, known as the "Army of the West," were to conduct the campaign in the northern provinces of Mexico, especially in New Mexico and California. Emory's party traveled from Fort Leavenworth to San Diego, arriving at the coast in December, 1846. His report to Congress was fully illustrated but contained only one view of a California scene, that of Old Town, San Diego. The sketch shows a few homes grouped around the plaza, those of José Antonio Estudillo, Juan Bandini, and Juan Machado being the most prominent. After 1851, when William Heath Davis and Alonza Horton became interested in the development of San Diego, the city grew around a new center more conveniently located on the bay and Old Town lost its importance.

WILLIAM F. SWASEY, of Maine, came to California in 1845 with the Snyder-Blackburn party. He worked for Sutter as an assistant bookkeeper and in 1846 went to Monterey, where he acted as clerk for William H. Davis and later became secretary to Thomas O. Larkin. During the Mexican War Swasey served with the California Battalion as assistant commissary in the southern campaign. At the conclusion of the war he was elected secretary to the Town Council of San Francisco. It was presumably during that time that his drawing of San Francisco was made. Fortunately it was lithographed in 1886, as the original was destroyed in the San Francisco fire of 1906.

The key to the picture, which appears on the lithograph, follows: *A*, U.S.S. "Portsmouth." *B*, U.S. Transports Ships, "Loo Choo," "Susan Drew," and "Thomas H. Perkins." *C*, ship "Vandalia"—merchantman consigned to Howard & Mellus. *D*, Coasting Schooner. *E*, Launch "Luce," belonging to James Lick. *1*, Custom House. *2*, Calaboose. *3*, School House. *4*, Alcalde's Office. *5*, City Hotel owned by Wm. A. Leidesdorff. *6*, Portsmouth Hotel. *7*, Wm. H. Davis Store. *8*, Howard & Mellus Store. The old Hudson Bay Co's building. *9*, W. A. Leidesdorff's Warehouse. *10*, Samuel Brannan's Residence. *11*, W. A. Leidesdorff's Cottage. *12*, First Residence of the Russ family. *13*, John Sullivan's Residence. *14*, Peter T. Sherback's Residence. *15*, Juan C. Davis' Residence. *16*, G. Reynolds Residence. *17*, A. J. Ellis Boarding House. *18*, Fitch & McKurley's building. *19*, Capt. Vioget's Residence. *20*, John Fuller's Residence. *21*, Jesus Noe's Residence. *22*, Juan N. Pidillas's Residence. *23*, A. A. Andrew's Residence. *24*, Capt. Antonio Ortega's Residence. *25*, Francisco Cacerez's Residence. *26*, Capt. Wm. Hinckley's Residence. *27*, Gen. M. G. Vallejo's building. *28*, C. L. Ross' building. *29*, Mill. *30*, Capt. John Paty's Adobe building. *31*, Doctor E. P. Jones' Residence. *32*, Robert Ridley's Residence. *33*, Los Pechos de la Choco. *34*, Lone Mountain. *35*, Sill's Blacksmith Shop. ⟫⟶ Trail to Presidio. ⟵⟪ Trail to Mission Dolores.

Yerba Buena. 1846–1847

Artist: WILLIAM F. SWASEY

From the lithograph published in 1886 by the Bosqui Engraving and Printing Co.

PLATE 21

THE AMERICAN FLAG was raised over the plaza of Yerba Buena on July 8, 1846, by Captain Montgomery of the United States sloop of war *Portsmouth* under orders from Commodore Sloat, who had taken possession of Monterey on July 7th. In January, 1847, the name of the town was changed to San Francisco, the plaza received the name of Portsmouth Square, and the street nearest the water front became Montgomery. The community had grown slowly in the ten years since Vioget's painting, "Yerba Buena, 1837" (plate 13), which showed but two houses. Swasey's drawing, 1846–1847, shows some twenty homes, the Mexican customhouse, the City Hotel, the Portsmouth House, the Hudson's Bay Company's building and the Public School. The view was made from the bay and shows the United States ships of war the *Portsmouth*, the *Loo Choo*, the *Susan Drew*, and the *Thomas H. Perkins* at anchor. The paths or trails to the presidio and to the Mission Dolores are traced.

In 1886 William F. Swasey, the draughtsman of the pictorial map of Yerba Buena at the time of the American occupation, secured the signatures of three men—General Vallejo, Colonel Stevenson, and George Hyde—who attested that this was a true picture of the town in 1847.

Plate 22: Notes

ALFRED SULLY, son of Thomas Sully, the American portrait painter, was born in 1820. He graduated from the United States Military Academy in 1841, and as a second lieutenant was engaged in the major battles of the Mexican War. From 1848 to 1852 he was on duty in Monterey in the position of quartermaster. While in Monterey his marriage to Manuelita Jimeno Casarin, daughter of one of the prominent Spanish families, took place. Sully served with distinction during the Civil War and in 1865 was placed in command of an expedition against hostile Indians in the Northwest. He painted a series of pictures of the western forts in addition to the picture of the Army's headquarters in Monterey.

Street Scene in Monterey. 1847

Artist: ALFRED SULLY

From the original painting. Courtesy of the Bland Galleries, New York.

Monterey Calif.

PLATE 22

THE UNITED STATES formally took possession of California when Captain William Mervine, commander of the *Cyane* and the *Savannah*, acting under orders of Commodore Sloat, raised the American flag over the Monterey customhouse on July 7, 1846. California was under military and civil rule until admitted as a state in September, 1850, first under General Stephen W. Kearny, followed by Colonel Richard B. Mason, General Persifor F. Smith, and Brigadier General Bennett Riley. Colonel Mason established his headquarters in El Cuartel, thus making it the first American capitol in California. El Cuartel had been erected about 1840 as barracks for the Mexican soldiers. An outside stairway which led directly to Mason's office on the second floor was constructed by the Americans.

Artists and draughtsmen among the military and naval forces stationed in the towns and presidios recorded, in pencil sketches and paintings, places and events of the transition period. Of these William H. Meyer, William Rich Hutton, Joseph Warren Revere, and Alfred Sully made sketches of Monterey. The view of Monterey by Alfred Sully pictures the headquarters, El Cuartel, of the United States Army in 1847. The water color shows the south end of the building, with a view of the bridge on Munras Street.

JOSEPH WARREN REVERE, naval officer, writer, and general in the Civil War, was in California during the war with Mexico, and was in command of the party that raised the United States flag at Sonoma on July 9, 1846. He withdrew from the United States Navy in 1850 and lived for a time on a ranch near Sonoma. At the outbreak of the Civil War he entered the army as a colonel of New Jersey volunteers, and rose to the rank of general.

Revere's *Tour of Duty in California*, published in 1849, was illustrated with six sketches. They are "Monterey, Capital of California," "Quicksilver Mine near Santa Clara," "Monte Diablo from the Sacramento River," "Sutter's Fort," "A Ranchero Feat," and "A Pui Day."

Quicksilver Mine Near Santa Clara

Artist: JOSEPH WARREN REVERE

From a lithograph in Revere's *Tour of Duty in California*, 1849.

PLATE 23

THE NEW ALMADEN quicksilver mine, named for the Almadén mine in Spain, is located in Santa Clara County, fifteen miles from San Jose. In 1845 Andrés Castillero, a Mexican miner, recognized the vermilion with which the Indians painted their bodies as red cinnabar, and took steps to obtain the site of the deposit from the Mexican government. He was granted title to three thousand yards in all directions from the mine and promptly organized a stock company of twenty-four shares to finance his venture. Four shares were given to General José Castro, military *comandante* of California. When the American forces arrived in California, Castro withdrew to Mexico and sold his shares to Barron, Forbes and Company of Tepic. In 1847

Robert Walkinshaw, agent for Barron, Forbes, came to California to further the development of the mine; and later, Alexander Forbes spent a year at New Almaden. By 1850, quicksilver was being produced commercially, and at the height of its production, in the 1880's, New Almaden yielded almost one-fourth of the world's output. The mine continued to produce until recently.

Joseph Warren Revere in his book, *A Tour of Duty in California*, describes the mine as "on top of a high mountain and the ore is brought down on mules, the path being very precipitous. The ore is the red cinnabar and the quality is extremely rich." Revere includes a sketch of New Almaden as one of the six illustrations in his book.

53

PLATE 24: NOTES

VICTOR PREVOST, painter, lithographer, and photographer, was born in France in 1820. He drew on stone two views of San Francisco: one, "San Francisco Upper California in 1847," and the second, "San Francisco Upper California in January 1849." Prevost's views were lithographed by the firm of Sarony and Major, New York, by whom he was employed. The original oil painting from which he made the earlier lithograph is in the possession of the California Historical Society. He later spent some time in France studying art and while in Europe developed a wax film which on his return to New York he used successfully in photography. A collection of his early photographs of New York City are in the library of the New York Historical Society.

San Francisco. 1847

Artist: VICTOR PREVOST

From the original painting in the California Historical Society, San Francisco.

YERBA BUENA at the time of the American occupation was a village of a few houses and perhaps two hundred inhabitants. The town was entirely without defense, since the presidio had been abandoned by the Mexican government in 1835. The Mexican customhouse faced the plaza and the flagpole stood on the slope a hundred feet below. On July 8, 1846, Captain Montgomery landed a column of seventy marines from the *Portsmouth* and raised the American flag. Ten days later the *Brooklyn* brought in a shipload of over two hundred Mormon colonists led by Samuel Brannan, thus more than doubling the population. Tents were pitched on the plaza, hotels were built, and a school opened. On January 9, 1847, the *California Star,* the first newspaper to be published in San Francisco, appeared. The ship *Thomas H. Perkins* arrived on March 6, 1847, bringing Colonel Stevenson of the New York Volunteers and the first detachment of his regiment. The soldiers had enlisted for the duration of the war and were to be disbanded in California. Many became permanent residents of San Francisco.

CALIFORNIA
IN THE GOLD RUSH YEARS

Roads to California

PLATE 25: NOTES

EDWIN ALLEN SHERMAN was born on August 25, 1829, at North Bridgewater, Massachusetts. In 1845, when war with Mexico seemed imminent, he enlisted in the United States Army and served in Mexico for the duration of the war. When the war was over and news of the gold discovery came, Sherman helped organize a company of emigrants going to California. They crossed northern Mexico and arrived in San Francisco on May 24, 1849. Sherman set out for Sacramento, a three-day journey, and on the afternoon of June 2, made the sketch reproduced here. He tried mining in various parts of the gold district, but in late 1850 he took up residence in Sonoma, becoming city clerk under Mayor Mariano Guadalupe Vallejo in 1852. While living in Sonoma he drew "The Lowering of the Bear Flag and the Raising of the American Flag at Sonoma by Lieut. Joseph Warren Revere, U.S.N. at 12m. July 9, 1846," a retrospective picture either based on accounts he had read or copied from some contemporary painting of the scene. In 1854 he returned to Boston for a visit and the same year returned to California in company with Frémont. Sherman remained in the West for the rest of his life. He was active in pioneer circles and interested in Freemasonry. During his latter years he lived in Oakland, California, where he died on March 17, 1914.

Sutter's Fort, June 2, 1849

Artist: EDWIN ALLEN SHERMAN

From the original wash drawing. Courtesy of Mr. Allen Sherman.

PLATE 25

ANY STORY of the gold rush period must begin with Sutter's Fort, the headquarters of Captain John Augustus Sutter. Sutter was a Swiss soldier-of-fortune who had seen much of the world but had acquired none of its goods when he arrived in California in 1839. His only assets were a genial personality, a persuasive tongue, and a warm heart. He found he could obtain free land by becoming a Mexican citizen. At the junction of the American and Sacramento rivers, on eleven square leagues of land granted him by California's obliging Governor Alvarado, and using credit advanced by trusting acquaintances, Sutter set up a combination ranch, fort, and trading post. The site he chose was at the head of navigation and in the path of overland emigration. Within a square of adobe walls his men built bunkrooms, kitchens, storerooms, granaries, and all the housing necessary for an independent community. Outside the enclosure they planted crops and ran cattle. Mounted cannon protected the establishment. "Sutter's Fort," as it was called, was soon known to Western trappers and traders as a supply center where they could obtain groceries, buy fresh horses and mules, or repair their equipment. More and more it came to be a sort of rendezvous point for overland emigrants.

The present city of Sacramento grew up around Sutter's Fort.

PLATE 26: NOTES

JOHN HENRY DUNNEL (sometimes spelled Dunnell) was born in Millbury, Massachusetts, in 1813. In 1847 he exhibited a picture at the National Academy of Design, and the following year showed two pictures, although painting was for him a recreation rather than a career.

When gold was discovered in California, Dunnel crossed the Isthmus and took the first regular steamer of the Pacific Mail Steamship line, the *Oregon*, to San Francisco. The *Oregon* arrived on April 1, 1849, and Dunnel went directly to the mines. He was in business at Coloma when California became a state, and was elected Coloma's first Justice of the Peace under the new state law. Early in 1851 he returned to New York City, where he became active in Republican political circles. He was an intimate friend of John Charles Frémont and took an active part in Frémont's presidential campaign in 1856.

In 1857 Dunnel made a second trip to California, this time as agent for the Singer Manufacturing Company. He stayed three years, maintaining an office in San Francisco, and then returned to New York City, where he remained for the rest of his life. He was a member of the New York Pioneer Association and an ex-member of the San Francisco Pioneer Association. The three pictures of Sutter's Mill which he drew when he first came to California are the only pictorial records of his western visit. At his death in 1904 his daughters inherited his pictures.

Sutter's Mill, April 1849

Artist: JOSEPH HENRY DUNNEL

From a photograph of the original pen and ink drawing. Courtesy of the Frick Art Reference Library, New York City.

PLATE 26

D URING THE 'forties the tide of emigration into California rose steadily, occasioning a constantly increasing demand for provisions at Sutter's Fort. The demand for flour was particularly heavy. A flour mill was needed to grind Sutter's wheat, but there was no lumber on hand from which to build one. The nearest good yellow pine was growing across the valley in the foothills along the American River. Captain Sutter sent his foreman, James Wilson Marshall, to select a place near the timber for a sawmill in which to cut lumber for a flour mill. The mill site chosen by Marshall was about forty-five miles from Sutter's Fort in a little valley on the South Fork of the American River, near an Indian village called Culloma. At a curve in the river Marshall's men dug a diversion ditch and put up a small sawmill. The mill wheel was hung too low and in order to deepen the mill-race Marshall allowed the water to run through freely during the night. In the morning the water was shut off and work resumed. Marshall's cursory examination of the bottom of the race on the morning of January 24, 1848, revealed shining flakes which he and Sutter tested and found to be gold.

PLATE 27: NOTES

JOHN HOVEY and a group of his home-town friends in Salem, Massachuetts, were in too great a hurry to get to California to wait for space on one of the regular ships. They formed themselves into a company, pooled their money, and bought the brig *Charlotte* so they could start at once. They left New York on January 23, 1849, with a shipload of cargo which they planned to sell in San Francisco. They arrived in San Francisco on July 23, and found the place a madhouse. They set up camp in Happy Valley, somewhat removed from the wild confusion around the Cove, and started repairing the *Charlotte*. The market was glutted with supplies and they had to give their cargo away to get rid of it. Dissension among the members of the company led to its dissolution and each man set out for the mines on his own.

Hovey was in the mines for nearly two years, trying first one location and then another, but without ever making a good strike. He found mining "a confounded hard way to make a living," and on May 30, 1851, he sailed for home on the *Constitution*.

Hovey's manuscript journal of his trip to California and his experiences in the mines is in the Henry E. Huntington Library at San Marino, California. It is illustrated with several rough drawings, including one of the brig *Charlotte*, reproduced here, and one of Sutter's Fort.

The Brig Charlotte, January 23, 1849

Artist: JOHN HOVEY

From the original water color in the Henry E. Huntington Library, San Marino, California.

SUTTER AND MARSHALL hoped to keep the gold discovery a secret until they could formulate some plan for handling the situation to their own advantage, but the story spread like a grass fire. Within a few days everyone in California had heard it. From California it was carried by ship across the Pacific to Hawaii, up the west coast to Oregon, south to Mexico, around the Horn to the east coast, and across the Atlantic Ocean to Europe. A local excitement became a world commotion. Men asked just one question: "What is the fastest way to California?"

Going by way of the Horn had some advantages for those living on the Atlantic coast. It took longer than other routes—one hundred and twenty days at sea—but it was relatively safe.

Although a ticket cost about $300, this expense was offset by the seeming certainty of finding a fortune in California. Thousands of young men stampeded the New York shipping offices demanding one-way tickets to California. All available space was quickly sold out and reservations booked for months ahead.

Shipbuilders on the Atlantic coast were quick to see the profits to be made from this great emigration round the Horn and within a year or two had put a whole fleet of fast clipper ships into service. But until the crowds of gold seekers were thus taken care of, many a brig such as the *Charlotte*, pictured here, was bought or chartered by small private companies for the trip to the gold fields of California.

PLATE 28: NOTES

CHARLES CHRISTIAN NAHL was born in Cassel, Germany, on October 13, 1818. His half-brother, Hugo Wilhelm Arthur Nahl (usually referred to as Arthur Nahl), was also an artist, as were his father and grandfather. In 1849 the two brothers left Paris, where they had been studying art, and went to New York. After a few months there they set out for California by way of the Isthmus of Panama. Charles made sketches of the trip from which he later painted several canvases. When the Nahls arrived in San Francisco in 1850 they found the excitement over gold still raging. They joined the crowds going to the mines, and prospected on the Yuba River, but after a few months Charles gave up mining and made an effort to establish himself as a painter in Sacramento. There was little interest in art in Sacramento and in 1852 he opened a studio in San Francisco.

Although much of the time between 1850 and 1867 was spent in earning a living by photography (a field in which he and his brother were pioneers) and commercial art assignments, Nahl also produced in those years many of the paintings for which he is remembered in Western art annals. In 1867 he secured Judge E. B. Crocker as patron and did a number of large canvases for him. During the 'seventies Nahl's pictures were much in demand and he accumulated a modest fortune. When he died on March 1, 1878, art critics wrote long columns in the daily newspapers, praising him as California's outstanding painter of pioneer life.

Reference has been found to a bound volume of Nahl's Panama sketches but no copy of such a book has been located. Except for "Chagres," which is reproduced in Perham Nahl's *Souvenir* (1878), these pictures are known only through printed reports.

For additional notes on the artist, see plates 31 and 48.

Chagres, 1850

Artist: CHARLES CHRISTIAN NAHL

From Perham W. Nahl, *Souvenir: Early Days in California,* 1894.

THE ROUTE across the Isthmus of Panama was shorter than the trip around the Horn, and thousands of emigrants chose to go that way because it took less time, although it was known to be a difficult, hazardous journey. The first part of the trip was pleasant enough— sailing down the eastern coast to the gulf town of Chagres. There the troubles began. Chagres was a tropical village of bamboo huts situated in a swampy glade, and had the name of being the most unhealthy place in the world. Most travelers going through carried life insurance but the policies contained a clause stating that to remain overnight in Chagres would constitute a forfeiture of coverage. Each traveler had to make his own arrangements with the natives for transportation up the Chagres River to Las Cruces or Gorgona. The wily natives asked exorbitant prices for their services, and often, after accepting payment in advance for the passage, would disappear, leaving the stranded emigrant to begin bargaining all over again with a different boat owner. A system was finally worked out whereby the emigrants would take possession of the boats they wanted, usually agreeing to pay eight dollars for each passenger and three dollars per hundred pounds for baggage, only half the amount being paid in advance.

The picture shows a party of emigrants seated in a flatboat called a "bungo."

Plate 29: Notes

Albertis del Orient Browere was born March 17, 1814, at Tarrytown, New York. He was the son of an obscure sculptor, John Henry Isaac Browere, whose chief claim to fame rests on his invention of a method of making masks from living subjects. Young Browere helped his father in this work but soon abandoned any idea of becoming a sculptor. He began to paint, following as nearly as he could the style of the Hudson River school. In 1831 he exhibited a picture for the first time, at the National Academy of Design. The next year he won a silver medal at the American Institute of New York for the best original painting.

His father died in 1834 and Browere moved to Catskill, New York, where he built a small studio in his backyard and supported himself by clerking in a drug store and painting signs. He continued to study and to paint in his leisure time and occasionally had a picture exhibited at local galleries. In 1852 he set out for California by sailing vessel.

Browere's "Crossing the Isthmus" was originally owned by Theodore F. Payne of San Francisco and in 1885 was presented by Payne's son to the Society of California Pioneers. Evidently it did not become a part of the permanent collection of the Society, for in 1933 it appeared in a group of paintings offered for sale by a New York gallery under the title, "Going to California."

For additional notes on the artist, see plates 38, 44, 50, and 68.

Crossing the Isthmus

Artist: Albertis del Orient Browere

From the original oil painting. Courtesy of Mr. Everett Lee Millard.

PLATE 29

THE TRIP from Chagres up the river terminated either at Gorgona or at Las Cruces, Las Cruces being the head of navigation. At these points baggage was transferred from the boats to the backs of mules, if any could be obtained, and the emigrants rode or walked from there across the Isthmus. An ancient trail paved with stones had once connected Las Cruces with Panama but it was now dilapidated and dangerous. From Gorgona the trail was even worse. The branches of a dense forest of trees arched overhead, at times entirely excluding the sun, while the thick underbrush pressed in on both sides. Deep chuckholes worn by the feet of mules made the going hard for man and beast.

Although the months from December to June were considered to comprise the dry season it was only during February, March, or April that the traveler could be sure of little or no rain and only then was the Gorgona trail traversable.

At first the natives were friendly and coöperative and sold the travelers eggs, meat, and rice at reasonable prices. But as the migration across their country assumed the proportions of an invasion they became resentful and alarmed. They refused to help in the transportation of goods, leaving travelers to shift for themselves as best they could. Heavy rains, poor mules, tropical heat, and myriads of mosquitoes made this part of the journey extremely uncomfortable.

DANIEL W. NASON of Epping, New Hampshire, was a member of the New England Pioneer Association of Boston, a group of fifteen young men described as "respectable young gentlemen who will go [to California] armed with the proper defensive weapons and take with them a tent." They left New York on the *Crescent City* on February 5, 1849, crossed the Isthmus, and caught the *Niantic* to San Francisco. While aboard the *Niantic* Nason made the sketch reproduced here. This is the only known picture of the famous old ship under sail.

In California, Nason mined at Mormon Island, Oregon Canyon, Jamestown, and other locations in the mining district, staying in California until 1852. At intervals he sent sketches east. A number of the sketches appeared as illustrations in the 1851 issues of Gleason's *Pictorial and Drawing-Room Companion*, among them the following: "A Winter Encampment of Gold Diggers between Oregon and Illinois Canyons"; "A Miner's Cabin, Thanksgiving Day"; and "View of the Mining Settlement and Modes of Working at the Southern Mines, Jamestown, California."

Nason was a member of the New England Association of California Pioneers in Boston and in 1891 he gave the association a portfolio of his California drawings.

Deck of the Ship Niantic, at Sea

Artist: DANIEL W. NASON

From Gleason's *Pictorial and Drawing-Room Companion*, August 30, 1851.

THE FIRST party of gold seekers to cross the Isthmus reached Panama just as the old whaler, *Niantic,* was loading for San Francisco. She had been withdrawn from the whaling trade and refurbished, her owner foreseeing greater profits to be had from a Panama–San Francisco passenger run than from the whaling business. She carried 248 passengers on that first trip—which proved to be her last as well—and arrived in San Francisco Bay on July 5, 1849. The anchorage off Yerba Buena Cove had been gradually filling up with vessels from every country, drawn there by the gold discovery, until by the time the *Niantic* arrived the bay was almost solid with deserted ships. As soon as the *Niantic*'s anchor was down the captain and all hands cleared out for the mines.

Many of the abandoned ships were floated over the mudflats to the edge of the cove and converted into stores and warehouses. After some months the *Niantic* was placed at the corner of Clay and Sansome streets and used as a warehouse. On May 4, 1851, the upper structure burned. The Hotel Niantic was built on the site, the charred hulk of the old ship serving as a foundation for it. This hotel was one of San Francisco's landmarks until 1872, when it was torn down to make way for stores.

PLATE 31: NOTES

DOUBT has been expressed as to whether this crude painting could be the work of Charles Nahl, although it is signed with his name, but contemporary reports give what seem to be conclusive proof that it is. In 1851, Paul Morrill, a Sacramento publisher, wrote:

> I saw some paintings that Nahl had hung up in a barroom. They were rough but mighty good . . . One was a very large scene of a family crossing the plains—and a team. One of the oxen had broken down and the old fellow was bringing some water to him. The women and one or two children were in terrible distress. It was so well pictured that it struck me it was a very nice thing. There was no finish about it. It was coarsely done.

And in the San Francisco *Daily Alta* for September 10, 1858, the following appears:

> Two large panoramic pictures by Nahl are . . . the same ones that were exhibited at the State Fair in Marysville. These two far surpass all else at the Fair . . . The first one is a scene of emigrants crossing the desert, brought to a sudden halt by the giving out of their cattle; one has lain down in its yoke to die. There are ten figures in the picture. One is offering water to the animal in a basin; the young girl on his right with hands clasped . . . ; other figures are grouped about. The dog, a gaunt skeleton, eyes protruding . . . bleak sands stretching away . . .

The size of the painting—16 by 10 feet— checks with the size given in an article in the Sacramento *Daily Union* for September 16, 1859. The picture is signed "Charles Nahl" in block letters, the usual signature on all of his early paintings (he later wrote his name in script).

"Crossing the Plains" was once owned by J. O. Coleman of Sacramento. It was eventually purchased by Mrs. Leland Stanford and is now in the collection of Stanford University. The photograph from which the engraving was made was obtained from *Life*, *Time*, and *Fortune*.

For additional notes on the artist, see plates 28 and 48.

Emigrant Family Crossing the Plains

Artist: CHARLES CHRISTIAN NAHL

From the original oil painting at Stanford University.

PLATE 31

ALTHOUGH THOUSANDS of gold seekers went around the Horn or across the Isthmus, a much greater number went overland. The usual point of departure was Independence, Missouri. From there the long-known trails of the early trappers and fur traders ran westward. One went southwest to Santa Fe, where the trail forked, one fork going through the desert and the other going by way of South Pass in the Rockies, both ending in southern California. Another route stretched from Omaha to Laramie and Fort Bridger, then crossed the Sierra Nevada and down the valley, in to Sutter's Fort, the trail's western terminus.

The familiar route of the United States Army across northern Mexico was used by the veterans of the Mexican War and by those living in the Southern States. All along the western trails there were trains of "prairie schooners" moving toward California. The wagons were covered with heavy canvas and seated as many as six people. They were loaded with provisions for a hundred-day journey and as much household equipment as space permitted. Inexperience led many of the immigrants to overload their wagons with nonessential goods, with the result that many teams broke down before reaching the Sierra Nevada.

PLATE 32: NOTES

JOHN WOODHOUSE AUDUBON, son of the great naturalist, John James Audubon, was born at Henderson, Kentucky. His father's long-standing ambition had been to make a trip west to continue his study of American birds, and when in 1849 John was invited to go to California as a member of Webb's California Company it seemed a splendid opportuty to carry out his father's plans. John signed the papers of agreement, naïvely thinking that his duties as commissary would leave him at least half his time for collecting birds and making drawings of them.

The company left New York on February 8, 1849, and proceeded to New Orleans, thence across Texas and northern Mexico to San Diego, which they reached in December, 1849. Upon reaching the gold fields the company dissolved. Audubon visited Wood's Diggings, Hawkins' Bar, and other locations in the southern mines. On April 16 he wrote: "I have made nearly seventy careful sketches and many hasty ones, the most interesting I have been able to find in these southern mines." Before he sailed for home in July, 1850, Audubon dispatched a portfolio of sketches which reached New York safely, but which has since disappeared. Another portfolio was lost at sea. All that remains of this artist's work is a few pictures in private collections and thirty-four unfinished sketches in the Southwest Museum.

Audubon carried on the work of publishing his father's *Birds of America* after his return from California. He died at the family home in New York City on February 18, 1862.

A Forty-niner

Artist: JOHN WOODHOUSE AUDUBON

From the original water-color drawing in the Southwest Museum, Los Angeles, California.

74

PLATE 32

THIS "USED UP" horseman was a member of Colonel Henry L. Webb's California Company, an overland party that went to California from New York by way of New Orleans and northern Mexico. The hardships he suffered were similar to those endured by hundreds of other Argonauts. The company was composed of Eastern "tenderfeet" who had no frontier knowledge, outfitted in heavy woolen uniforms unsuited to the climate of the Southwest. When some of the men died of cholera on the banks of the Rio Grande, many of the others, including Colonel Webb, the leader, were frightened into deserting. Those that continued on were robbed by the natives of Monterrey and ran out of pro-visions in the mountains of northern Mexico. Their mounts were so poorly secured at night that they were frequently missing by morning, and precious hours, often days, were spent rounding up the strayed mules and horses. When the bedraggled party finally reached San Diego after a six months' journey they were reprovisioned by the United States Army garrison stationed there and sent on their way up the central valleys of California to the gold fields in the Sierra Nevada foothills. By the time they arrived they found that thousands of others, there ahead of them, had taken all the best claims. As far as is known not one of the ninety men of the California Company made a "pile" in the diggings.

California at Last!

PLATE 33: NOTES

THIS IS ONE of six oil paintings of exceptional interest and high artistic merit painted by Frederick Tobin in 1850. The pictures are on Whatman paper and measure approximately twenty by fifteen inches. They are unsigned and undated.

The only clue to the artist's identity is contained in a dealer's note in an auction catalogue which reads: "The following statement was pencilled on the back of one of the old frames from which this and the following four paintings were taken: 'Painted by Fred Tobin, 1850, recently Secretary to the Society of Foreign Artists.'" A search through contemporary San Francisco directories and art catalogues has failed to turn up any further information about this artist.

The paintings are now the property of Mrs. Celia Tobin Clark of San Mateo, having been purchased at auction in New York and presented to Mrs. Tobin by her father-in-law, Senator Clark.

San Francisco. Looking East from Clay and Powell Streets

Artist: FREDERICK TOBIN

From the original painting. Courtesy of Mrs. Celia Tobin Clark.

PLATE 33

S AN FRANCISCO was the port of entry for the great throng that came to California by sea in '49. As the ships carrying the emigrants rounded Telegraph Hill, the town gradually came into view. From the water it appeared to be no more than a sprawling village on the edge of a cove, backed by a semicircle of chaparral-covered hills. Vessels had to anchor well out in the bay, for there was no deep-water pier at which they could be accommodated. Passengers and cargo were taken ashore in small boats to a wharf at the foot of Clay Street. This was the general unloading place for every type of merchandise imaginable, with barrels and packing boxes piled and thrown about in utter confusion. Along the water front and scattered part way up the sloping hillsides were wooden and sheet-iron houses of every kind, shape, and description, and tents of every color. The center of town, if it can be said to have had one at this early date, was an old adobe customhouse facing the public square, a short distance up the hill. Constantly milling around this spot was a floating population of gold seekers, adventurers, merchants, speculators, gamblers, deserting sailors, and refugees from justice, whose number was augmented daily by two or three hundred. Some slept on sandhills at the outskirts of the town.

PLATE 34: NOTES

ARTISTIC ability of the quality displayed in "Russian Burying Ground" was not often present in gold rush California. Most of the men upon whom we are now dependent for a graphic record of the gold rush period were not trained artists, but amateur daubers of little or no talent. Yet their productions depicted so many phases of life in California that even though countless items have now disappeared it is still possible to reconstruct a pictorial record of the times from those that are extant.

Fortunately there was a handful of professional artists attracted to the west coast, for one reason or another, whose work was not only historically important but aesthetically pleasing as well. The unknown Frederick Tobin was one of these talented few.

Russian Burying Ground

Artist: FREDERICK TOBIN

From the original painting. Courtesy of Mrs. Celia Tobin Clark.

PLATE 34

I N THE FIRST MONTHS of the gold rush there were several unofficial, casual burying grounds and scores of single graves scattered about Yerba Buena Cove. It was necessary to bury corpses as quickly as possible and graves were often dug behind the most convenient clump of greasewood or in some empty lot. Some graves were marked with a thin flat board or a rude cross, but most of the mounds were unmarked. There were a number of graves on the southern slope of Telegraph Hill, grouped in a spot tacitly set aside for the purpose; others were placed in a plot of ground near North Beach.

Catholics were buried in consecrated ground near the old Mission Dolores. On the summit of Russian Hill was a small unenclosed cemetery older than the others and known as the Russian Burying Ground. It is believed that the first graves dug there were those of four Russian otter hunters who were killed in a clash with the Spanish authorities in 1809, although according to another account the graves are those of men brought ashore from a scurvy-ridden Russian ship.

By 1854 all traces of the Russian Burying Ground had been obliterated.

PLATE 35: NOTES

EDWARD BOSQUI was born in Montreal on July 23, 1832. His formal education ended at the age of eleven, when he started working in a bookshop. In 1850 he went to California, where he found employment with Palmer Cook and Company, bankers. While with this firm he came to know all the prominent residents and visitors in San Francisco, among them Colonel and Mrs. John Charles Frémont, Alexis Godey, Jose Y. Limantour, and Samuel Brannan.

In the 'sixties Bosqui started what was to be his lifelong occupation, printing, and the Bosqui Engraving and Printing Company became, in time, one of San Francisco's largest printing houses. Always anxious to promote the cultural growth of San Francisco, and being an amateur artist himself, he befriended many of the young artists of the city and was one of the organizers of the San Francisco Art Association.

Bosqui's extensive collection of pictures by California artists was lost when the Bosqui home in Marin County burned in 1897. Bosqui suffered another disastrous loss when his printing establishment was completely destroyed in the fire of 1906. He was not again active in business and died at his home in San Francisco on December 8, 1917.

Samuel Brannan's Residence in San Francisco

Artist: EDWARD BOSQUI

From the original water color in the Society of California Pioneers, San Francisco.

PLATE 35

FROM THE TIME of its erection in 1846 until its destruction by fire in 1851 this house was one of the more important dwellings in San Francisco. It was built by Captain Stephen Smith of Bodega on a fifty-vara lot located at what later became the southwest corner of Dupont and Washington streets. The redwood lumber of which it was built probably came from across the bay near Saucelito. It was a story and a half high, with a long portico, and was one of the few buildings in the little village having any architectural style. In August, 1846, Samuel Brannan became its tenant.

Brannan was the leader of a colony of two hundred Mormons who arrived in San Francisco on July 31, 1846, aboard the *Brooklyn*, and he immediately became one of the dominating personalities in the new community. He leased Captain Smith's house and installed his family in it. He had brought with him a complete press, and on January 7, 1847, he issued the first number of the *California Star*. This was San Francisco's first newspaper and the second to be published in California. The house continued to be headquarters for the Brannan family and the press while numerous business ventures called Brannan to other parts of the state. It was sometime in May, 1849, just outside this house, that Brannan, returning from the newly discovered gold fields, waved his hat and gave the now historic cry that is said to have started the gold rush: "Gold! Gold from the American River."

PLATE 36: NOTES

GEORGE HOLBROOK BAKER was a native of Massachusetts, born at East Medway on March 9, 1827. He was apprenticed to an artist in New York and at the time of the gold discovery was a student at the National Academy of Design. He joined a group going to California by way of Mexico and arrived in San Francisco in May, 1849. In June he made an elaborate drawing of "The Port of San Francisco," which was published in the New York *Tribune* for August 28, 1849. Baker immediately went into the mercantile business in Sacramento but his main interest continued to be sketching. His diary entry for July 6, 1849, reads:

> I have made ten sketches since I arrived in California. This afternoon I am to make a view of this place (Sacramento) from the opposite side, having the offer of some artistic materials for my trouble. I yet hope to be able to pursue my original intention of illustrating California in a manner it deserves. But my first care must be to get the means which will enable me to do this. Nothing can be done without money . . .

The view he was to make from the opposite side of the river was for Mr. Benjamin T. Martin, who, in 1886, had George A. Frost make an oil painting from it. The painting by Frost is now in the California State Library.

During the 'fifties Baker engaged in a number of business ventures in Sacramento but spent a great deal of his time in sketching the mining towns. In 1862 he moved his home and lithographic business to San Francisco, where he continued to work as an artist and lithographer until his death in January, 1906.

For additional notes on the artist, see plate 69.

Sacramento, July 6, 1849

Artist: GEORGE HOLBROOK BAKER

From a photograph of the original drawing in the California Historical Society, San Francisco.

84

Sacramento City July 1849

PLATE 36

SACRAMENTO CITY was originally planned by Captain Sutter to center around his fort, two miles from the river, but as Sacramento became the main outfitting depot for the northern mines, the merchants moved close to the river for convenience in receiving and housing incoming cargoes. There was no embarcadero. Passengers and supplies were discharged directly on the raw embankment. All the chaos of a growing frontier town manifested itself in Sacramento. An unending stream of horse, mule, and human traffic passed through the streets, going and coming from the mines. Before the close of '49 there were gambling dens and saloons by the dozen, a sprinkling of street preachers, an occasional temperance lecturer, circus troupers, teamsters, storekeepers, fortunetellers, assayers, lawyers, prostitutes, and plenty of business for everyone.

This view shows all there was of Sacramento in July, 1849—the water front between J and K streets. At the left the framework of the three-story City Hotel is faintly discernible behind the trees. The first ship at the left was Hensley & Reading's storeship, the *Guipuscoana;* the next ship was Samuel Brannan's *Eliodora,* moored near his store, and farther to the right, the brigs *Elvira* and *Saltillo.*

THIS PICTURE of Stockton was painted by Captain Josiah Perkins Cressy of Marblehead, Massachusetts, in 1849, for Captain Charles Weber, at whose home Cressy was a visitor while his ship was laying in supplies in California, en route to India. Captain Cressy, born in 1814, was a master mariner in the great days of the China tea trade when a captain's skill in handling a clipper made the difference between profit and loss for his company.

He was the master of the *Flying Cloud* on its initial voyage in 1851, when a record of 89⅔ days' sailing time between New York and San Francisco was made. Cressy made the same run five different times but equaled this first record only once, on the fourth trip, arriving in San Francisco on April 20, 1854, 89⅓ days from New York. On his last voyage in 1855 the ship struck a coral reef in the China Sea and would have foundered had not Captain Cressy floated her off successfully. Upon his return to New York he left the sea for a number of years. When the Civil War started he joined the merchant marine as captain of the *Archer*, bound for China. The ship put in at San Francisco in April, 1865, and Cressy was given a royal welcome-home by his many friends.

The picture shown here was copied in 1856 by Carl E. Grunsky, an early resident of Stockton and a clever artist. Grunsky's copy has been reproduced in Volume X of the Society of California Pioneers *Quarterly*. The original painting is in the possession of Captain Weber's descendants and is reproduced here for the first time.

Stockton, 1849

Artist: JOSIAH PERKINS CRESSY

From the original painting. Courtesy of Mrs. Margaret Kennedy.

PLATE 37

STOCKTON (first called Weberville or Tuleburg) was settled by Captain Charles M.
Weber in 1847 on land granted him by the
Mexican government. The San Joaquin River
was navigable to the point where Captain Weber
established his embarcadero. In October, 1849,
when this picture was painted, Stockton was
a muslin-and-shake town straggling along the
levee. During the years of the gold rush a flourishing inland port city grew up around this spot.

From the right-hand side of the picture to
the left, the buildings shown are: Grayson and
Stephen's store (at the corner of what became
Center and Levee streets), E. Lane's store, the
Stockton Shades Saloon, Alcalde George Belt's
tent-office, a two-story framework that became
the United States Hotel, the California Restaur-
ant, and the Stockton office of Adams' Express
Company. Sundry old schooners, barks, and
brigs are shown tied close to the shore, where
they served as stores and warehouses, one being
used for city hall, jail, and hospital. The cargo
piled here and there was waiting transportation
to the mines. All the flimsy buildings shown in
the picture, as well as many of the old hulks,
went up in flames on Christmas Eve, 1849.

At the Diggings

PLATE 38: NOTES

IN THE San Francisco *Daily Alta* of January 26, 1852, the following notice appeared:

California lithographs:—We have received from Mr. C. A. Shelton, the publisher, 2 lithographs, drawn and executed in very good style in this city and representing scenes in the life of a California miner. They appear to be the commencement of a series. One represents the cabin of some miners at the close of the day . . . and the other a miner, with his horse and pack mule, starting on a prospecting expedition. They are drawn on stone by C. Nahl and A. Wenderoth and lithographed by B. F. Butler.

A. Wenderoth was Charles and Arthur Nahl's brother-in-law. He came to California in 1850 with the Nahls and was associated with Charles Nahl as a lithographer and daguerreotypist. Albertis Browere met them in San Francisco and undoubtedly saw their painting of the propector. In 1853 he painted his own version. The two pictures are identical except that Nahl's prospector is riding a white horse and leading a pack mule, there is a knife in his boot top, and he carries a large bedding roll instead of a pick and shovel.

The Nahl and Wenderoth picture has been reproduced several times, but as far as is known the Browere version is reproduced here for the first time.

For additional notes on the artist, see plates 29, 44, 50, and 68.

The Lone Prospector

>   *Artist:* ALBERTIS DEL ORIENT BROWERE,
>   after a painting by Charles Nahl
>   and A. Wenderoth

From the original oil painting. Courtesy of Mr. Everett Lee Millard.

THE MINING region lay in the foothills of the Sierra Nevada across the valley from the river towns of Stockton and Sacramento. Before setting out for the mines from these last settlements the Argonauts made their final purchases of equipment. The minimum essentials for a prospecting trip in the mountains consisted of food, a blanket roll, pan, pick, shovel, and a good sidearm or two. The guns were usually brought along from the east coast. The proper clothing, including a red flannel shirt, a large soft hat, and heavy-duty boots, was usually bought in San Francisco. The mining tools were purchased in Stockton or Sacramento. Travelers to and from the mines either walked, rode a horse or mule, or hired a wagon and team, depending upon their means and preference. By far the most common method of travel was by mule.

"FERRY ON THE TUOLUMNE," an original oil painting, was presented to the California State Library in 1947 by the Stanislaus County Free Public Library, to which it had been given by a descendant of Peter Nye, who stated that it was a painting of the ferry at Don Pedro Bar. Although it is not dated, verification of the dates when the Nye and Lewis ferry was in operation places the scene as not later than 1857. No clue to the artist's identity has been found.

A Ferry on the Tuolumne River

Artist: Unknown

From the original oil painting in the California State Library, Sacramento.

PLATE 39

FERRYING became a popular way to get rich quick as soon as it was seen that thousands of persons and animals would be on the trails that connected the various mining districts. The ferry shown in this picture was located where the trail from Stockton to Sonora crossed the Tuolumne River at Don Pedro Bar. At this important river crossing there was a settlement of considerable size in the middle 'fifties, when Peter Nye and Daniel C. Lewis owned the ferry and the hotel. General Ulysses S. Grant's description of Knight's Ferry on the Stanislaus River in 1852 might have been written of Nye and Lewis' ferry on the Tuolumne, or of any number of other river ferries operating profitably in California in the early years of the gold rush:

Their ferry, which is managed by two persons, is drawn across a little river about 150 feet wide, by ropes attached to both shores. It takes about one minute from the time they leave one shore until they reach the other. The charge is $2.00 which is much less than they formerly got. In connection with this is their tavern, or, as it is called, "The Knight's Ferry House" where the passengers by stage and many teamsters stop and get a dinner at one dollar. They have stables which the stage companies pay them about $200 per month rent for and board all their men with them at $10 per week. They have a trading house [and] a ranch . . .

PLATE 40: NOTES

LITTLE is known about J. Lamson, and had not a portfolio of his sketches and his manuscript journal survived, his California visit would be unrecorded. He first came to California on the *Sarah Eliza,* arriving in San Francisco on July 2, 1849; at some time after 1852 he returned to his home in Sebec, Maine, but made a second trip to California in 1856. His manuscript journal records his stay in California from 1856 to 1860.

During this time he traveled extensively throughout the mining region, not as a miner, but as an itinerant artist. He made innumerable sketches at the request of the California pioneers—mine owners would ask him to make a drawing of their claims; proud home owners wanted sketches of their California houses and grounds to send east to their families. Occasionally Lamson tried mining or storekeeping but such ventures were of brief duration and he returned to sketching. His journal and portfolio of sketches are now in the collection of the California Historical Society.

For further notes on the artist, see plate 57.

Emory's Crossing

Artist: J. LAMSON

From the original water color in the California Historical Society, San Francisco.

PLATE 40

B Y THE mid 'fifties the rough trails and the crude ferries connecting the more populous mining districts were for the most part replaced by privately owned toll roads and toll bridges. Although there was a great deal of dissatisfaction over the expense and inconvenience of paying tolls, the toll roads were the only ones that were not "a perfect jelly of mud and slush" in spring or a suffocating cloud of dust in summer, and the public, traveling to and from the mines, had no choice but to use them and to pay for the privilege.

Thornton C. Emory's toll bridge over the Middle Branch of the Yuba River, four miles above Freeman's Crossing, was advantageously located near the junction of three main trails. One led up Oregon Creek to Downieville, a second turned right across the creek to Alleghany, Forest City, and Henness Pass, and a third proceeded by the Moonshine Road to Bullard's Bar. Connor & Wentworth's tri-weekly stages from Nevada City to Downieville and Langton's Express from Marysville to Forest City passed over Emory's bridge. In addition to owning the bridge and a stretch of turnpike, Emory also had a hotel and store at the crossing. His various businesses prospered from 1853, when the first wagon road between Downieville and Nevada City was completed, until 1862, when his bridge was swept away in the spring flood.

WILLIAM M'ILVAINE was born June 5, 1813, at Philadelphia, and graduated from the University of Pennsylvania in 1832. After graduation he traveled extensively in Europe, studying art. By 1840 his European pictures were being exhibited by the Artists' Fund Society of Philadelphia. He moved to New York City about 1845 and left from there early in 1849 for a visit to the California gold fields. He arrived in San Francisco in June and went directly to the mines, going from Sacramento to Stockton, thence by way of Wood's Creek to the Tuolumne and Merced rivers. He sketched along the way and seems to have been more interested in the scenery than in the mining operations. He returned to San Francisco and left for New York on November 1, 1849. The record of his brief visit to California is contained in his book of sixteen plates and text, *Sketches of Scenery and Notes of Personal Adventures* (1850).

"Scene on the Tuolumne" was exhibited in 1854 and again in 1858 at the Pennsylvania Academy of Fine Arts, along with his "Prairie in California."

Scene on the Tuolumne

Artist: WILLIAM M'ILVAINE, JR.

From the original oil painting. Courtesy of Kennedy Galleries, New York City.

PLATE 41

Panning was the first and simplest method of obtaining gold used in California. All the equipment required was a shallow pan ten to fourteen inches in diameter and a shovel. Panning was successful only along the streams where the richest gold deposits were to be found. The dirt directly above bedrock was the richest, and as bedrock was usually from four to seven feet down the miners had to strip off the top soil before getting to "pay dirt." Pay dirt was clay, sand, gravel, loose slate, or silt containing enough gold to make it profitable to wash it. Bucketfuls of it were carried to the edge of the water, the pan was partly filled with dirt, lowered into the water, and there gently swirled with a rotary motion. The soil, clay, or sand was thus carried away, leaving the gold on the bottom of the pan. An experienced miner could tell from the first panful if the claim would pay. If the pan showed a ten- to twelve-cent prospect the claim was considered worth working. It was not unusual for one man to wash out enough gold to fill an oyster can in half a day, even though the panning method was slow and wasteful and much of the gold was carried away by the water.

Although some of California's most beautiful scenery was to be found along the Tuolumne River, this view must be considered an artist's idealized conception of a prospector's claim somewhere on the river between Jacksonville and Hawkins' Bar in the summer of 1849.

GEORGE NAPIER, about whom we know nothing, sent the sketch which is reproduced here to his father in England in July, 1849. The sketch and the following letter were published in the *Illustrated London News,* November 17, 1849:

> . . . Our party made two machines by felling an oak tree, splitting it and hollowing it out . . . Our work for the week done by four men amounts to $212, being $53 to each man; our expenses including tools, cradles, and provisions $104, or $26 to each man. Our tools and cradles will last us for a long time. Gold is worth here $16 an ounce; but at San Francisco $17 an ounce is paid for it. This work of ours is thought very bad here as $16 a day is called the average, and I have seen men working within a few feet of us make two or three ounces apiece a day. Some of our company have made six ounces a day.

Such letters and sketches were printed as front page news in English and Continental journals during the height of the California gold excitement.

Gold Washing at the Diggings

Artist: GEORGE NAPIER

From the *Illustrated London News,* November 17, 1849.

PLATE 42

P ANNING was much too slow and tedious a method to suit Yankees who wanted to make their pile in a hurry and be on their way home again. The laborious washing of the dirt by the panful continued to be used for prospecting but for the working of a claim the pan was soon replaced by a device known as a cradle, or rocker.

The cradle was operated by hand. It was made like a trough, either of boards or by splitting and hollowing a tree trunk, an opening being provided at the lower end to allow the water to run off. A sieve of iron mesh or a perforated sheet of wrought iron was attached to a removable frame and on this was thrown the dirt to be washed. Water was then poured on and the mixture stirred thoroughly. The larger pebbles and rocks were picked out. The gravel, sand, and gold fell through the sieve and the gold, being the heaviest, was caught and retained by means of cleats nailed across the bottom of the trough. The advantage of the cradle over the pan washing was that a greater quantity of dirt could be washed at one time. The cradle was the ideal machine for two men working in partnership since each could keep steadily at work, one digging and carrying the earth in a bucket and the other washing and rocking the cradle. In one day two men could wash from a hundred to a hundred and fifty cubic feet of dirt, depending on the type of soil being washed. Shallow diggings near a plentiful supply of water were easiest to work.

Plate 43: Notes

THE NAME of the artist who made this gouache drawing, which is dated 1853, is unknown. It was purchased in France in 1929 by the Kennedy Galleries of New York and has since been in their possession.

Many relics of California's gold rush are found in France. This is not surprising, as the number of immigrants from France exceeded that from any other foreign country with the exception of Mexico. It has been estimated that there were twenty thousand Frenchmen in California in 1851.

Between 1848 and 1854 France was suffering from a serious economic depresssion. To many Frenchmen the California gold fields seemed a way out of their troubles. Alluring stories of the great wealth to be had in California appeared in French newspapers, inspired by various promotional organizations; widely distributed lithographs and engravings showed how easy it was to pick up nuggets along the California rivers. By September, 1849, shiploads of Frenchmen were on their way to California.

They infiltrated the entire mining region but settlement was heaviest in Calaveras County, particularly near Mokelumne Hill. Antiforeign sentiment was so strong that many French and Mexican miners were driven off valuable claims. In 1850 the California Legislature passed the Foreign Miners Tax Law and this discrimination and continued persecution caused many of the French miners to leave the mines. When the situation became known in France, migration was much reduced.

Calaveras River: Miners at Work

Artist: Unknown

From the original gouache drawing. Courtesy of Kennedy Galleries, New York.

PLATE 43

AN OUTGROWTH of the rocker and an improvement over that method of extracting gold from pay dirt was the Long Tom. A Long Tom was an open-ended trough, about two feet wide at the upper end and twice that at the middle. From the middle to the lower end the bottom was made of perforated iron, ending in a snub-nosed upward curve. A second trough, called the riffle box, was placed directly under the trough having the perforated bottom. This lower trough had cleats nailed across the bottom, and water was turned into the upper end. A crew of three or more men was needed to work a Long Tom. Two men shoveled dirt into the upper section while a third man constantly stirred the mixture. The larger rocks remained in the upper trough while the finer particles of gravel, sand, and gold fell through into the riffle box. Most of the gold was caught on the cleats but the Long Tom was not entirely efficient, since some of the finer particles escaped. In order to reduce this loss several Long Toms were sometimes placed in a series along a river bank, in order to subject the dirt to several washings and screenings. It would appear that the artist intended to show such an operation in the picture.

PLATE 44: NOTES

THE OIL painting, "Placer Mining," 26 by 36 inches, signed A. D. O. Browere and dated 1854, was one of two pictures by Browere in the Edmund L. Gould collection when that collection was sold by a New York art dealer in 1933. The second picture by Browere in the Gould collection was a large oil painting of Columbia, also dated 1854. These pictures, together with several others by the same artist, were exhibited in 1940 at the M. H. de Young Memorial Museum in San Francisco.

Beside the pictures reproduced or mentioned here, there are a number of Browere's large oil paintings of California scenes in art galleries and in private collections, including the following: "The Falls of the San Joaquin," "Valley of the San Joaquin," and "Scene near Sutter's Mill."

For additional notes on the artist, see plates 29, 38, 50, and 68.

Placer Mining

Artist: ALBERTIS DEL ORIENT BROWERE

From the original oil painting. Courtesy of Mr. Everett Lee Millard.

PLATE 44

By the summer of '49 every accessible gulch and stream bed in the Mother Lode district was being prospected and mined. Changes in methods of mining were being made so rapidly that often, along the same stream, several kinds of operations, from pan washing to dredging, could be seen going on at the same time.

Blasting and moving boulders to clear the ground for prospecting, digging and carrying dirt for washing, or felling trees for cradles and Long Toms required a great deal of hard labor and was usually undertaken by men working in partnership. The number of men in a partnership varied according to the type of mining under way. Two or three men could work a simple placer claim by panning, but seven or eight men were needed to operate a string of Long Toms. Mining partnerships were usually temporary arrangements for the working of a specified claim and could be dissolved without formality.

In the painting "Placer Mining" the faces are portraits of men who were in the mining region at the time. The man holding the pan is believed to be the artist himself.

PLATE 45: NOTES

THIS PICTURE of Kanaha Bar was sent back to England by the artist, John David Borthwick. It was published in the *Illustrated London News*, January 24, 1852, with the following editorial comment:

Of the many illustrations of this new Gold Field which the obliging intelligence of Correspondents has enabled us, from time to time, to present to the readers . . . the large view upon the preceding page presents the most practical picture. It has been sketched by Mr. John Borthwick, a clever water colour painter, who first visited the locality as a gold-seeker but is now settled in the neighbourhood, and is actively engaged in his profession, by taking portraits of successful adventurers, chiefly to be sent to their friends at a distance . . . Besides presenting us with a picture our ingenious Correspondent has sketched with equal minuteness the industrial economy of this extraordinary scene.

It is probable that more than one picture by Borthwick was published in the *Illustrated London News*, but a search of early issues failed to turn up any others signed or attributed to him by name. In addition to the eight illustrations in his *Three Years in California* and the Kanaha Bar scene, the following California pictures by Borthwick are known: "Stockton, Main Street" (two views); "Interior of a Miner's Cabin" (an oil painting); "View of Mokelumne Hills" (a lithograph); "Dead Broke" (an oil painting exhibited at the Royal Academy in 1862); and "The Miner's Grave" (an oil painting exhibited at the British Institute in 1865).

For additional notes on the artist, see plate 52.

Kanaha Bar

Artist: JOHN DAVID BORTHWICK

From the *Illustrated London News,* January 24, 1852.

PLATE 45

AFTER the river bars had been thoroughly worked over with pan, cradle, and Long Tom, miners' attention turned to the possibility of getting at the gold that was believed to lie on the river beds.

The only way to expose the river beds was to divert the water from its regular course by means of wing dams and flumes. This required a great deal of labor and capital and could be undertaken only by men working in large groups. These groups were usually organized as joint stock companies, the work and the expense being shared by all. During the summer of 1850, when this type of river mining was in full swing, so many miles of wooden flumes were built that the hills were almost denuded of timber. It took months of labor to build the flumes and the wing dams, and only after they were completed and the water turned into the flumes could mining be started in the exposed beds.

A project of this kind could be undertaken only in the summer months when the rivers were low, and consequently the mining day during this season began at dawn and ended at dark. In spite of such feverish activity the work was seldom completed before the rainy season set in. The first heavy rain raised the river, broke the dams, and washed away the summer's work.

PLATE 46: NOTES

WILLIAM NEWTON BARTHOLOMEW was born in Boston, Massachusetts, on February 13, 1822. His father tried to make a farmer of him but he preferred to draw. He had no teacher but developed his own talent through study and practice.

In 1850 Bartholomew accompanied J. Wesley Jones on a daguerreotyping expedition overland to California. In the course of this extraordinary undertaking several hundred daguerreotypes of overland scenery and the mining towns of California were made. When the party returned east a corps or artists made pencil sketches from the daguerreotypes and then enlarged those sketches on canvas for a huge panorama. The panorama was enthusiastically enjoyed by capacity houses in Boston and other eastern cities.

After his marriage in 1876 Bartholomew's home was in Newton Centre, Massachusetts. He spent his life teaching drawing in the Boston schools and painting landscapes in his leisure time. He was the author of several books on the technique of drawing and was a member of the Boston Art Club. In 1891 and 1892 he exhibited at the Pennsylvania Academy of Arts. He died at his home in 1898.

The Phoenix Dredging Machine

Artist: WILLIAM NEWTON BARTHOLOMEW

From the original pencil sketch in the California Historical Society, San Francisco.

PLATE 46

Turning a river out of its bed was a laborious and costly task and one that had to be repeated every time the dams and flumes were swept away by floods. In the search for more efficient methods of obtaining gold from the river beds, dredging was tried.

Eastern capitalists organized companies to dredge the rivers for gold and sent dredgers to California for that purpose. One of the most extensive dredging operations attempted in California was tried by the Yuba River Gold Dredging Company in the fall of 1850. In spite of local skepticism the company set up the *Phoenix,* with its steam-driven machines, dredge, and rockers, six miles below Marysville. When it was found that the machine could not be operated at a profit in that location it was moved higher up the Yuba, to the vicinity of Cigar Bar, one of the richest locations on the river. The owners believed that the deposits of gold there would undoubtedly have paid a profit had it not been for the exorbitant cost of operating heavy machinery in a country like California. Although the *Phoenix* was actually run at a profit for a short time in January, 1851, in the long run it was found, like most of the machines, to dredge more money from the pockets of the owners than it did gold from the rivers. The use of dredgers was abandoned until late in the century, when lower cost of operation made their use feasible.

PLATE 47: NOTES

THOMAS A. AYRES left his native New Jersey on February 4, 1849, aboard the *Panama*, with the first rush of gold seekers, and arrived in San Francisco on August 8, 1849. Although his activities during his first year in California are unrecorded it may be safely assumed that he followed where thousands led—to the "diggings." Certainly he was living at Tuttletown in the early days of that camp's existence. Ayres soon found that for him a brush was a more profitable tool than a pick and at the end of a year he returned to San Francisco with a portfolio of sketches of the gold rush towns and the mining country. From 1850 until 1854 Ayres traveled over the state, sketching and painting. In 1855, when James Mason Hutchings, a San Francisco journalist, organized the first tourist party ever to visit Yosemite, he took Ayres with him to make sketches of the valley to be used as illustrations in his *Illustrated California Magazine*. Ayres made thirteen sketches, which were the first pictures ever made of the Yosemite Valley. From them Ayres painted an enormous panorama which had a long and successful run at McNulty's Hall in Sacramento. Approximately eleven of the original drawings are preserved in the Yosemite Museum.

For additional notes on the artist, see plates 55 and 59.

Miner's Cabin at Tuttletown, April, 1852

Artist: THOMAS A. AYRES

From a photograph of the original water color at the California State Library, Sacramento.

108

PLATE 47

THIS "MANSION" in the mountains was a snug little structure of canvas stretched over uprights and was made habitable in winter by the large fireplace. The chimney was built of mud and stones and topped by an empty barrel for a chimney pot—a popular architectural practice in the mining districts. The cabin faced the main street of Tuttletown, and can be seen in Ayres' drawing of that village (plate 59).

In the summer a light tent or *ramada* (a brush-covered shelter open on three sides) provided adequate shelter—many miners slept in the open—but when the rains began in the fall, work on the claims stopped and the miners either went down into the valley towns or "holed up" for the winter, in whatever habitation was available. Those who had log cabins were fairly comfortable but in sections where the timber was scarce canvas shelters had to serve. Many of these canvas houses were made out of sails looted from abandoned ships in San Francisco Bay. The one shown in this picture was occupied by the artist, Thomas Ayres, and his friend, A. L. Tashiera, in April, 1852.

PLATE 48: NOTES

THE OPINION held by some that Nahl's pictures of early California were not painted until the 'seventies is contradicted by the evidence. The block-letter signature on this painting and on "Emigrants Crossing the Plains," the date 1856, and the following description from the *Sacramento Daily Union* of September 16, 1859, offer definite proof that at least these two pictures were contemporary with the scenes they depict:

> There are six persons in the cabin. Through the open door of the cabin the moon is shining and from the sill a winding stream can be seen. One of the party is engaged in cooking over a large fire; one is already half seas over in the enjoyment of the contents of a bottle which he clasps in his left hand, one is weighing out the week's or day's "dust"—an operation which is closely watched by two others of the party. The bunk is already occupied by a sleeping member of the company.

"Saturday Evening in the Mines" measures 16 by 10 feet. It was first displayed in a saloon at the corner of Third and K streets in Sacramento, and was exhibited at the State Agricultural Society's fair in 1859. J. O. Coleman of Sacramento once owned the picture and it was purchased from him by Mrs. Leland Stanford. It is now in the collection of Stanford University.

The pen and ink drawing reproduced on the title page was one of the early sketches made by Nahl after his arrival in California. It is reproduced by courtesy of Mr. George A. Pope, San Francisco.

For additional notes on the artist, see plates 28 and 31.

Saturday Evening in the Mines
Artist: CHARLES CHRISTIAN NAHL

From the original oil painting at Stanford University.

PLATE 48

TEMPORARY canvas shelters and unchinked log structures provided the miners with shelter adequate for the warm summer months in the mining region, but from October until May more permanent covering was desirable. Men wintering in the mines lined their log cabins with clapboards to make them weatherproof. A bark roof kept out the rain. A split log served as a door. The interiors were scantily but sturdily furnished with crude homemade furniture. A wooden frame with a canvas stretched on it and a mattress of straw or leaves served as a bed. Tables were nailed together from rough boards. Wooden kegs or three-legged stools were used for seats. Cooking was done over the open fire of the mud and stone fireplace. A pot and a frying pan were the only necessary cooking utensils. The one piece of fine equipment that might be found in a miner's cabin would be a delicately balanced pair of gold scales.

Life in such a setting was primitive, and often, as in this picture, crowded. Here six men are confined within one small room. The evening chore of weighing the gold dust is in progress while the cook for the day prepares the evening meal. These men were probably, as was often the case, banded together by a verbal agreement to work a claim in joint partnership.

PLATE 49: NOTES

THIS SKETCH of Ophir was made in the fall of 1851 by Chauncey Langdon of Vermont, who come to California by way of the Horn in 1849. He mined near Ophir for a time and later went into farming at Rohnerville, Humboldt County. While living in the vicinity of Ophir he was engaged by Joseph W. Gregory to make sketches of Ophir and Auburn, two of Gregory's express depots. The drawings were lithographed and then published by Gregory as the front page of a double letter-sheet, for advertising purposes. Only the Ophir view is reproduced here. The only known copy of this letter-sheet is in the M. H. de Young Museum at San Francisco. A photographic copy from the collection of Boutwell Dunlap hangs in the Freeman Hotel at Auburn.

Gregory's Express at Ophir, Placer County
Artist: CHAUNCEY LANGDON

From the pictorial letter-sheet. Courtesy of the M. H. de Young Memorial Museum, San Francisco.

PLATE 49

THE ARRIVAL of the express, bringing news from the rest of the world and letters from home, was an event of great importance to the isolated camps and towns in the mountains. The expressman was the connecting link between the miners and the world "down below." On his way out of the mountains he carried the miners' mail, packages, and gold dust.

A network of independent express companies operated throughout the mining districts in the early years of the gold rush. Joseph W. Gregory's Express was one of the first of these lines. He made an auspicious start in April, 1850, with agents at Mormon Island, Coloma, Auburn, Ophir, Placerville, and other camps, and soon expanded to cover an even larger part of the mining region. Gregory was the first to use a light wagon for collections wherever roads permitted. His advertisement in the San Francisco *Daily Alta* of April 1, 1850, read: "Gold dust forwarded and insured to New York and small parcels forwarded by each steamer. Also messages, packages, and parcels delivered at the mines." Rival express companies soon invaded Gregory's territory, giving him keen competition. The number of lines multiplied and services were extended throughout the area—even to the most remote mining camps. Each line offered the fastest service, the best equipment, and the lowest rates. Although Gregory had been the pioneer in several small mountain towns the difficulties of competing with larger capitalists led him to sell out to Wells, Fargo & Company in November, 1852.

PLATE 50: NOTES

BROWERE'S FIRST trip to California was a four months' journey in a sailing ship around the Horn in 1852. He went to the mines more as an observer than a miner, and later put his impressions of mining life on canvas.

Browere returned to his home in Catskill, New York, in 1856. In less than two years he was again on his way to California, this time going by way of the Isthmus. In San Francisco he was active in civic affairs but except for an allegorical painting which he did for the Odd Fellows' celebration in 1859 there is no record that he painted any pictures during the three years of his visit. After his return to New York in 1861 he painted a succession of landscapes, Biblical scenes, fruit pieces, etc., but his greatest contribution at any time was in the field of "Americana," pictures of everyday occurrences.

"The Miner's Return," an oil painting, is signed A. D. O. Browere and dated 1854. The canvas measures 24 by 30 inches.

For additional notes on the artist, see plates 29, 38, 44, and 68.

The Miner's Return

Artist: ALBERTIS DEL ORIENT BROWERE

From the original oil painting. Courtesy of Mr. Everett Lee Millard.

PLATE 50

A MINER'S LIFE was a hard one. He was among strangers in an unknown wilderness, and was usually totally unfamiliar with even the simplest methods of mining. Dreams of easy money, to be had just for the picking up, soon faded under the grim reality of actual prospecting. In addition to the physical labor involved there were the sufferings and hazards attendant upon life on the frontier, and the knowledge that his chance of striking it rich was a matter of mere luck. Many a man walked, disheartened and empty-handed, over ground that yielded millions to those who came later.

Perhaps the worst thing the California forty-niner had to bear, however, was a gnawing homesickness that kept him a hopeless victim of what was known as "home-bound" fever. The mail pouches from California to the East were heavy with letters expressing the longing to go home. Only the reluctance to return without a "pile" kept thousands from giving up and returning to their families.

PLATE 51: NOTES

WILLIAM S. JEWETT was an established portrait painter in New York when, in 1849, he decided to go to California as a member of a mining company. The mining company dissolved almost as soon as it arrived in San Francisco, and Jewett, after disposing of his interests in the company, opened a small one-room studio on Clay Street. He was twice burned out in San Francisco fires but each time began again. His particular talent lay in portraiture and as men began to accumulate fortunes from California gold and to establish homes in San Francisco Jewett's business prospered. By the middle 'sixties he was San Francisco's most popular and fashionable portrait painter. He painted portraits of Alcalde Washington A. Bartlett, John C. Frémont, Colonel Collier, and many other notables, and his full-length portrait of Captain Sutter was purchased by the state legislature in 1855 for $2,500.

Jewett's landscapes were fewer in number but well done. A view of Culloma, painted in 1851 for his friend, J. J. Little, brought him $600. The view of Hock Farm reproduced here was painted in 1852 and at that time was known as "A View of the Buttes from Hick [sic!] Farm Ranch, California." It is an oil painting, 29 by 40 inches.

Jewett had planned from the first to return east to his home but again and again postponed the visit. It was not until 1869 that he finally went east. He died at Springfield, Massachusetts, on December 2, 1873, leaving a considerable estate earned by his brush in California.

Hock Farm. 1852

Artist: WILLIAM S. JEWETT

From the original oil painting in Sutter's Fort Historical Museum, Sacramento.

PLATE 51

HOCK FARM, which took its name from an Indian village near by, became Captain Sutter's home and refuge from 1849 until 1865. Sutter moved there when the great influx of gold seekers made life intolerable and property unsafe at his fort. The ranch had been established in 1841 on a fertile plain bordered by the west bank of the Feather River, about eight miles below the present site of Marysville, where the fields were high enough to insure floodless grazing grounds for cattle. A beautiful redwood mansion was built in 1849, and adobe outbuildings and corrals were erected. Vineyards, orchards, and gardens of rare plants and shrubs were set out.

Sutter's troubles pursued him. His cattle were stolen and at one time a large number of his horses were driven off to Oregon. Squatters overran his land and carried their claims to court, starting a long battle over the legality of Sutter's titles. A decision by the United States Land Commission in favor of Sutter was reached in 1857, but a year later the Supreme Court declared certain of his titles invalid. Hock Farm began to be eaten up by debt and attachments. He was still clinging to it when on June 7, 1865, a small band of vindictive men believed to have been representing the squatters set fire to the house. Sutter and his family escaped but the house and all it contained burned to the ground.

Gold Rush Towns (Ghost Towns of Today)

PLATE 52: NOTES

JOHN DAVID BORTHWICK was born in Edinburgh, Scotland, the son of Dr. George Borthwick. John David and his elder brother George attended the Edinburgh Academy where they distinguished themselves as scholars. The Borthwick home was next door to that of the artist Robert Inness. It is probable that the young John Borthwick received art instruction from either Inness or an Edinburgh portrait painter also named John Borthwick. His subsequent work indicates not only native talent but early and expert instruction.

In 1840 John's brother left the family home for Canada and a few years later John went to New York. In 1851 he started for California by way of Chagres, and arrived in San Francisco, the "city of rats, fleas, and empty bottles," in September. The story of Borthwick's visit to California is related in his *Three Years in California* (1857). Borthwick was both intelligent and observant. He moved his residence with the ease of an Arab, visiting nearly all the camps of the mining district. Part of the time he earned his way by drawing crayon portraits of people who wanted to send their pictures home to their families. From California Borthwick went to Australia. In 1857 his book was published in Edinburgh. From 1860 to 1870 he lived in London where he practiced his profession and was a member of the Royal Academy.

For additional notes on the artist, see plate 45.

Our Camp on Weaver Creek

Artist: JOHN DAVID BORTHWICK

From Borthwick, *Three Years in California*, 1857.

PLATE 52

THE HOPE of finding better diggings kept the gold seekers constantly on the move, following the streams up the canyons, going higher and higher into the mountains, prospecting every likely spot as they went. At night their tents were pitched in the wilderness, often miles from any settlement. Such a camp was that of Borthwick on Weber Creek. (Borthwick called the stream "Weaver," using the Mexican pronunciation for "Weber.")

It was near here that Captain Charles M. Weber did his first mining and trading. Early in the summer of '48 he organized the Stockton Mining and Trading Company at Tuleburg (Stockton) to mine along a tributary of the South Fork of the American River. They located a claim a few miles from Hangtown (later Placer-

ville) and called the stream Weber Creek. It was a very rich location, the gold being found in medium-sized particles of particularly fine quality. Captain Weber's friend, José Jesús, chief of the Stanislaus Indians, supplied Captain Weber with Indian workers for the claims. Captain Weber not only mined but also ran a brush-covered store on the banks of the creek, where he traded goods for gold dust. Weber's success in mining and trading attracted hundreds of men to the area and numerous communities grew up along the creek.

Although evidences of early mining activities may still be seen in the canyon and along the banks of Weber Creek, the sites of Borthwick's camp and the settlement of Weberville have disappeared.

PLATE 53: NOTES

BAYARD TAYLOR was born at Kennett Square, Chester County, Pennsylvania. As a young man he was interested in art and engraving and asked John Sartain to instruct him. The request was refused, since Sartain was not then taking pupils, and Taylor turned his attention to writing.

In 1849, when he was writing for the New York *Tribune*, the editor, Horace Greeley, told him "to go west, young man" as a roving reporter. Taylor arrived in San Francisco in September, there met and talked with everyone of importance, and then toured the mining regions. He attended and reported the first constitutional convention at Monterey. The articles that he sent east to his paper were among the most informative and interesting accounts of the day. The entire series was used later in his book, *El Dorado, or Adventures in the Path of Empire* (1850). It was illustrated with a sketch of San Francisco made by James C. Ward and several of Taylor's own drawings.

Taylor built up quite a reputation as a lecturer in the East and in 1859 he was asked to make a lecture tour of California, which he did. His attention turned to the diplomatic service and in 1862 he was appointed secretary of the legation at St. Petersburg; in 1878 he was made United States Minister to Germany. He died on December 19, 1878.

Lower Bar, Mokelumne River

Artist: BAYARD TAYLOR

From Taylor, *El Dorado, or Adventures in the Path of Empire*, 1850.

Plate 53

A MEDLEY of Americans, Sonorans, Kanakas, and French were mining at Lower Bar on the Mokelumne River when Bayard Taylor visited the camp on October 13, 1849. The mining claims were in a canyon at a junction of the Mokelumne River with a dry gulch. The ground was extremely hard and the miners were turning it over with great labor. The Sonorans had their own way of "dry washing." They tossed the dirt repeatedly into the air and blew upon it as it came down, catching the heavier particles, which included the gold, dexterously in a basket. The rest of the miners were using water from the Mokelumne River, standing waist deep in the stream. The whole scene was one of feverish activity. On this particular day there was an added excitement in camp. It was California's first election day. Every man was vitally interested in obtaining the admission of California to the Union and the first step in that direction was the ratification of the newly drafted constitution. Even in such isolated spots as Lower Bar voting was in progress. Returns were carried from Lower Bar to Double Springs where the rider from Upper Bar picked up the combined returns of Lower Bar and Double Springs and took them to Stockton.

The exact location of Lower Bar, like so many other transient camps of the time, has long since been forgotten, but it is believed to be one of the camp sites now covered by the waters of Pardee Dam.

PLATE 54: NOTES

THE OIL PAINTING reproduced was made sometime between 1849 and 1854 and was the property of Mrs. Harriet Poor, whose husband Elijah ran the Natoma Hotel at Mormon Island. The picture has remained continuously in the family of the original owner. At some time in the past it was mounted in order to preserve it and in the process the name of the artist was covered up and forgotten. Speculation as to the artist's identy includes consideration of Albert Lyman, whose diary entry for September 25, 1849, reads: "Sketching and drawing of the Mormon Island and Village, from a hill on the north side"; Adolphe Boson and John A. Lee Martin, artists who were in Mormon Island in January 1850; and Daniel W. Nason, whose drawing of Mormon Island was published July 5, 1851, in *Gleason's Pictorial and Drawing-Room Companion*. There is also an unsigned drawing of Mormon Island in the Sacramento *Daily Union* of May 1, 1854.

Mormon Island

Artist: Unknown

From the original oil painting. Courtesy of Mrs. M. Hoxie.

PLATE 54

AT ALMOST the same time that gold was discovered at Coloma it was found on the south bank of the American River about twenty-five miles above Sacramento. This discovery was made accidentally by two Mormons who chanced to stop there for the night. Within a few weeks a camp had mushroomed up and claims were staked out until there was not room for another man. The mining ground consisted of a bar of gravel and earth deposited by the river on its south side. At a very early stage of operations a canal was cut through the bar, making an island from which the place got its name. The island was very rich. Gold was found in such quantities that it was measured by the pint and half pint.

When the peak of activity was reached in 1851 there were hundreds of miners' huts in the town and about twenty-five fair-sized buildings, including a post office, express office, several hotels, and an uncounted number of saloons, all flourishing. A decline set in when the gold became less plentiful and after a fire in 1856 which destroyed all of the buildings shown in the picture, the town was not rebuilt. A chicken ranch now occupies the public square of Mormon Island.

PLATE 55: NOTES

THIS DRAWING of Tuttletown was made by Ayres in April, 1852, while on his first visit to California. In 1857 he was commissioned to make a series of sketches of California Scenes for publication in *Harper's Illustrated Weekly*. He began his sketching tour in southern California, and visited San Diego, Los Angeles, and a number of outlying settlements. His tour completed, he boarded the *Laura Bevan* for San Francisco, carrying his portfolio of drawings with him. On the night of April 26 the ship and all aboard were lost in the heaviest storm of the season.

The disaster of the *Laura Bevan* terminated a career that was just beginning and one that would have been of increasing importance to California. The twenty or thirty pictures that Ayres made of California scenes are outstanding contributions to California's pictorial history.

For additional notes on the artist, see plates 47 and 59.

Tuttletown, April, 1852

Artist: THOMAS A. AYRES

From the original pencil drawing in the M. H. de Young Memorial Museum, San Francisco.

PLATE 55

Tuttletown, with famous Jackass Hill at its back, was once a flourishing trade center and pack-mule stop on the old Slumgullion road from Angel's Camp to Sonora. It is chiefly remembered now as the place where Mark Twain bought his groceries when he lived in the Gillis cabin on the hill. Twain probably had Tuttletown in mind when he wrote:

You will find it hard to believe that here stood at one time a fiercely flourishing little city, of 2000 or 3000 souls, with its newspaper, fire company, brass band, volunteer militia, bank, hotels, noisy Fourth of July procession, and speeches, bearded men of all nations and colors, with tables heaped with gold dust—streets crowded and rife with business—town lots worth $400 a front foot—labor, laughter, music, swearing, fighting, shooting, stabbing—a bloody inquest and a man for breakfast every morning—and now nothing but lifeless, homeless solitude. In no other land, in modern times have towns so absolutely died and disappeared as in the old mining regions of California.

Tuttletown, named for Anson Tuttle, one of the early arrivals on Mormon Gulch, was settled because of its placer deposits but the later discovery of rich quartz veins in the vicinity prolonged its mining life. Francis S. Marryat, an English journalist, artist, and soldier of fortune, was the first to set up machinery for quartz mining at Tuttletown. He hauled in an eight horsepower steam engine, causing great excitement and a rise in hopes among the miners. But Marryat's machine broke down and Marryat set out for San Francisco for new equipment. He never returned and the venture was abandoned. The town continued to have some mining activity for many years but after the 'sixties it steadily declined in size and importance until it finally disappeared altogether.

PLATE 56: NOTES

GEORGE H. GODDARD was born in Bristol, England, in 1817, and educated at Oxford. In 1852 he went to California and settled in Sacramento. Had there been a market for his drawings he might have established himself as an artist but the offers he received in the field of civil engineering seemed more promising financially. He received a number of assignments with government surveys, among them that of locating a practical wagon route across the Sierra Nevada. However, he retained his interest in drawing, hoping some day to publish a series of several hundred views of "California Illustrated." Goddard was disappointed in this ambitious plan but a number of his pictures were published as separate lithographs. Unfortunately for Goddard the lithographic stones were the property of the lithographer until the sale of the drawings paid the cost of lithographing them. As the drawings sold very slowly the lithographer often appropriated the stones and published a great many letter-sheet copies, making considerable profit at the expense of the artist.

During his long life as a civil engineer in California Goddard spent his leisure time collecting minerals, maps, and drawings of California. The entire collection burned in the San Francisco fire of 1906. Goddard died at his home in Berkeley a few months after this loss.

Campo Seco

Artist: GEORGE HENRY GODDARD

From a lithograph in the California Historical Society, San Francisco, California.

PLATE 56

CAMPO SECO was situated in the southern part of the mining district between Wood's and Sullivan's creeks about a mile south of Jamestown, and was the center of a flourishing locality of pocket mines. It was here in 1852 that the first and most ambitious attempt was made to bring water from distant sources to dry diggings. A canal was constructed through which the water from Wood's Creek was brought into Campo Seco; later a second ditch was dug so that there was always an abundance of water on hand. It was here also that the first successful use was made of the flume sluice box, an arrangement whereby a great quantity of dirt could be washed at one time by long lines of men standing on either side of the trough.

While its mines were producing the town flourished. It had one of the first theaters to be built in the county, a wooden-sided, canvas-roofed affair, hardly more than a tent, in which the Chapman family played. But the claims gave out after a short while and the town's population drifted away. A fire in August, 1854, almost totally destroyed the buildings, and except for a brief revival in the 1860's, when the Penn Copper Mine was located at Campo Seco, the place has had no further existence as a town. The site is marked by one or two stone ruins.

Plate 57: Notes

Lamson was keenly aware of the demand for pictures of California and similarly aware of his shortcomings as an artist. On January 12, 1856, he wrote in his journal:

Hitherto my attempts have been mere experiments, which have proved to be tolerably successful in winning the approbation of my employers; and I am induced to continue the business though deeply sensible of my entire ignorance of the art of drawing. Necessity compels me to exertion, and my attempts at other kinds of business having failed, I resolved to give this a trial. An ardent love of the beautiful in nature and some slight taste for drawing—though almost wholly uncultivated—and a desire to visit some of the beautiful and picturesque localities in California superadded to the hope of acquiring a little California gold, were the great inducements that tempted me to try this, to me, new and untried art. I was further encouraged to attempt that as a regular business by the good offices of a kind friend . . . and now, with the intention of wandering wherever interest or curiosity might lead me, I packed up a few articles of wearing apparel and some drawing materials and set out on my tour, which might as circumstances favored or discouraged, continue for months or terminate in a week.

To overcome his shortcomings as a painter he engaged George A. Baker, a Sacramento artist, to instruct him, but after a lesson or two decided to learn from a drawing book; he later took lessons from Mrs. Mary P. S. Benton in San Francisco. After these lessons he succeeded in selling some of his work to James Mason Hutchings for publication in Hutchings' *California Illustrated Magazine.*

For additional notes on the artist, see plate 40.

Bidwell's Bar

Artist: J. Lamson

From the original pencil drawing in the California Historical Society, San Francisco.

PLATE 57

BIDWELL'S BAR on the Feather River was a combination trading post and mining camp, first mined by John Bidwell early in 1848. Most of the men who formed the first camp on the bar were, like Bidwell, farmers who used their Indian farm hands to work the mines. The first houses were of cotton cloth and anyone who wished might easily have cut his way in any direction through the camp. When the miners started replacing their muslin houses with frame buildings they found the bar so rich that it was difficult to place the house foundations where there was not rich pay dirt. Bidwell's Bar was formally laid out as a town in 1853. A wire suspension bridge was ordered from Troy, New York, shipped around the Horn, and erected in December, 1855. Activity in the town was then at its height and the gold seemed inexhaustible, but in another twelve months the output began falling off. By 1857 Bidwell's Bar was in its final slump and when the artist Lamson stopped at the Shade Hotel in April he found nothing left but "a pleasant village on the south side of the Feather River with a pretty suspension bridge."

Towns That Survived the Gold Rush

CAPTAIN GRIPPEN was a member of the party led by Major Downie to the junction of the North and South forks of the Yuba River, where later the town of Downieville was built. Captain Grippen's sketch of Downieville and his reminiscences are interesting documents of life in an early mining camp:

I was one of the first to arrive there . . . and with Major Downie built the first cabin. Diggings proved very rich and soon a crowd of miners, merchants, traders, saloonists, hotel men and gamblers, erected a city . . . of cloth and pine shakes. It did not turn out to be a mushroom city but a stayer. Among the prominent names in those days was Uncle Ned the butcher who drove in abandoned cattle from the plains and sold us the beef at $1.50 a pound. Haskell was first postmaster. Langdere's [Langton's] Express brought up the mails and we were glad to get our letters at $2.00 each. Haskell ran a store and poker table in connection with the post office. Another old familiar was Bartell the pie man who built dried apple pies and sold them to us at $1.50 making his pile and going back to Vermont without wetting his feet mining. Uncle Ned furnished the tallow for shortening. First theatre was in '51, your humble servant being sole leasee and manager. Posters were printed with a brush upon brown wrapping paper costing 25 cents a sheet by W. S. T. Ballou, our scenic artist. We had a big jam filling the house and our pockets every night. But one night the grand edifice built of shakes and cloth burned down. No one perished in the flames fire escapes being on the ground floor . . . The biggest excitement . . . occurred when Galloway brought his wife in—the first American woman to come to Downieville . . .

Captain Grippen's view of Downieville is a piece of rare Californiana. It is believed to be the earliest view made of Downieville and there is but one known copy of the letter-sheet on which it appeared.

Downieville, May, 1851

Artist: A. W. GRIPPEN

From the pictorial letter-sheet. Courtesy of Dr. E. E. Rhoads.

PLATE 58

THE LETTER on the pictorial sheet reproduced here reads in part: "Downieville, May 9, 1851, Dear Brother Moses: I got a sketch of Downieville on this sheet, it is not perfect. You cannot see the mountains are on either side of the City. You must imagine mountains several thousand feet high covered with tall spruce and pine, the River is represented to be running swift . . . You can see a sawmill owned by Mr. Durgin from Ill. was formerly a contractor on the Canal. The large round tent is a gambling saloon where men make and lose fortunes the small house on the south side of the street and in the end near the pine tree was bilt by Thristin and sold for $400. The 8th House east of that on the same street was bilt by the Wightmans and Field and myself we have not sold it yet but rent it. Where you see the men amining is the bed of the nort fork. They have got large piles out of that place. Last fall when thay wair doing the best they avraged about 26 lbs a day for 2 wks on the flat One day they got 48 lbs. The flat South of the North Fork where you can see 3 or 4 windless was a very rich also, the South Fork is principally hid from your view. The man tat sketched this is one of the company that I am with. . . . Perhaps you imagine that you can see some ladies walking the street . . . there was but one whight woman at the fork when this was sketched. . . . News came the other day that San Francisco was burned to the ground . . ."

PLATE 59: NOTES

ONE OF THOMAS A. AYRES' major projects was the preparation of a series of views of California from which oil paintings were made and exhibited as a panorama, called "California on Canvas." A copy of the program of the panorama in the Bancroft Library at the University of California lists forty-six separate drawings with this note:

These views drawn from nature by Thomas A. Ayres, painted by Thomas A. Smith, are truly a California work of art. They form the most superb collection of oil paintings ever offered to the public and correctly represent California as it is. Painted expressly for exhibition in the Atlantic states and in Europe, it is believed they will add to the already high character of California abroad.

The artist's preliminary pencil drawings of several of the views named in the program are in the collection of the Society of California Pioneers—among them is "Sonora from the South," reproduced here. The oil paintings made from the drawings are believed to have been destroyed.

For additional notes on the artist, see plates 47 and 55.

Sonora, November, 1853

Artist: THOMAS A. AYRES

From the original drawing in the Society of California Pioneers, San Francisco.

PLATE 59

SONORA was built along the course of Sonora Creek in a little valley between two ranges of hills. The first camp was established by Mexican miners from the state of Sonora in the summer of '48. The Sonorans had their own method of dry washing and within the first few months took a great quantity of gold from the surrounding country, which finally yielded more than $40,000,000 worth. For several months the Mexicans were the sole occupants of this district, but by the summer of '49 the Americans had moved in and the camp became a small town. In 1850 the Mexicans were ejected by the American miners, but this action was later rescinded.

The city was officially organized in 1851. By this time there were buildings for a considerable distance on both sides of Stockton Street (along Sonora Creek) and on Washington Street, the area shown at the right-hand side of the picture. Three disastrous fires occurred between June, 1852, and October, 1853. As this view is dated November, 1853, much could be said for the tenacity of the Sonoran residents. New buildings, some of them three stories high—and not a canvas structure among them—had already taken the place of the burned ones.

Unlike many of the gold rush towns, Sonora did not cease to exist as a town when its mines gave out, although it never regained its early importance.

PLATE 60: NOTES

CHARLES L. PARRISH was born in New York, and in his youth served an apprenticeship to a builder and architect. In 1850 he went around the Horn to California, intending to work at mining. He soon concluded that mining provided too precarious a living and decided to take up more steady employment. He settled at Jackson, where he manufactured rock crushers and quartz mills, and the house which he built there is still standing. As a side line he sold carriages which were sent out from New York, and for several years he was also the owner of the toll bridge at Big Bar. About 1865 Parrish and his family moved to Oakland. He died in 1902 while visiting relatives in the East.

The few pictures he made were more nearly architectural delineations than artistic compositions. Three of his original drawings were sold in San Francisco in 1946: "Volcano," "Mokelumne Hill," and the view of Jackson reproduced here.

Jackson, Calaveras County, May, 1854

Artist: CHARLES LOUIS PARRISH

From a photographic copy of a lithograph. Courtesy of the California Historical Society, San Francisco.

PLATE 60

Some towns originated as convenient stop-over places on the main trails to the mines. One of these stopping places was on the road to the Mokelumne River mines at the junction of the forks of Jackson Creek. The place was at first called Botilleas, or Bottle Springs, because of the discarded bottles thrown there, but was later named Jackson, for Alden A. M. Jackson, a lawyer from New England, who had an office in the camp.

Jackson first boomed in 1850, when thousands of gold seekers swarmed along the trails, and again in 1854, when improved mining methods gave new life to the mining claims in its vicinity. With the sudden prosperity of '54 all the lawlessness of a frontier town came to Jackson. Saloons, gambling dens, and brothels ran full blast day and night. Robberies and murders were common. At last the citizens took matters into their own hands. The hanging of a criminal from the big tree on the main street became an ordinary and frequent event. Right or wrong, this method of dealing with outlaws quelled the worst elements and finally brought about law and order.

Plate 61: Notes

Arthur Nahl worked with his famous brother Charles, sharing a studio with him in San Francisco. Many of the pictures and designs that came from their studio were joint creations. Like his brother, he was a versatile artist, but he excelled at painting animals. The huge grizzly bear which he designed for the state flag is known to every Californian.

A number of Arthur Nahl's early wash drawings of California towns have been preserved, among them "Viacita, 1852"; "Springfield, 1852"; "Coloma"; "San Francisco in 1853"; and "Georgetown" (which is reproduced here). He was the illustrator of *The Oatman Children*, published in 1856. One of his drawings, "Pioneers Crossing the Sierra Nevada Mountains on Horseback," appears as an illustration in James Linen, *The Golden Gate* (1869).

During the 'seventies Nahl was a frequent exhibitor at the San Francisco Art Association. In 1888 he was awarded a silver medal at the California State Fair for his pictures in crayon and charcoal. Except for a trip to Europe in 1881, he remained in San Francisco until his death on April 1, 1889.

Georgetown, 1856

Artist: Arthur Nahl

From the original wash drawing. Courtesy of Mr. George A. Pope.

PLATE 61

GEORGETOWN had two claims to distinction among California gold rush towns: it was a planned town site and it was set upon a hilltop instead of in a valley.

The settlement was originally situated in a ravine along the course of a stream, the usual location for a mining camp, when mining operations were begun along the banks of Oregon Creek in Hudson's Gulch by a company from Oregon who arrived there in 1849. At this time the town was known as Growlersburg, and it might have remained in the canyon indefinitely had there not been a fire in 1852. The fire started in the Round Tent gambling den, where an ambitious photographer was trying to take a picture of a dead miner. The flames did not die out until the entire town of Growlersburg had been burned to the ground.

It was decided to rebuild at the top of the hill, on the dividing ridge between the South and Middle forks of the American River. The sugar pines were cleared away and a main street one hundred feet wide marked off. Former Growlersburg merchants and hotel men were given first choice of lots, the less desirable ones going to newcomers. The new town was named Georgetown, after George Phipps, the leader of the original settlers. The surrounding countryside was rich in placer mines and the new town flourished as a trading center for the neighboring settlements of Georgia Flat, Kentucky Flat, and Volcanoville. By 1855 it was a cultural center in the mountains, having a school, a church, a theater, and a town hall. The proud citizens referred to it as "Georgetown, the pride of the mountains."

PLATE 62: NOTES

ALEXANDER EDOUART, the founder of the California branch of the Edouart family, was born in London, England, on November 5, 1818. The date of his arrival in California is not known but his name first appeared in San Francisco directories in 1858, at which time his occupation was given as "printer." Between 1858 and 1861 he painted several California scenes, among them, "Santa Clara Valley Scene," "Dedication of the New Almaden Mine," "Sketch of Round Valley, Mendocino County, California," and "Mendocino Hunting Party." His "Fort Bragg" was made for his friend, Lieutenant Horatio Gates Gibson. Lieutenant Gibson (later General Gibson) gave the picture to his daughter, Mrs. Katherine Gibson White, who now owns it.

With the development of photography Edouart began the hand-coloring of photographs, a type of work much admired in the early 'sixties. Later he apparently stopped painting and devoted his entire time to photography, and in 1889 moved to Los Angeles, where his son was associated with him in a photography studio. Edouart died in 1892, but his son and a grandson are still carrying on the photographic business.

Fort Bragg, 1858

Artist: ALEXANDER EDOUART

From the original oil painting. Courtesy of Mrs. Katherine Gibson White.

PLATE 62

INDIAN POLICY on the West Coast followed the general pattern established in the East in colonial days. The Indians of California were gradually pushed off their ancestral lands and their hunting grounds appropriated by the incoming settlers. In the 1850's the federal government took action to protect the Indians and at the same time to prevent any depredations against the settlers. A number of small reservations were established throughout the state. Military posts were set up on each reservation in the belief that the presence of soldiers would prevent hostilities between settlers and Indians.

In 1857 Lieutenant Horatio Gates Gibson was ordered to establish a military post on the Mendocino Indian Reservation. The post was situated in a heavily timbered glade on the coast near the mouth of the Noyo River. It was named Fort Bragg in honor of a hero of the War with Mexico, General Braxton Bragg. The picture reproduced here shows Lieutenant Gibson (who was in charge of the fort during the first year of its existence) reviewing the twenty men of Company M, 3d Artillery.

The post at Fort Bragg was discontinued in 1864 and the lands thrown open to public purchase at $1.25 an acre. A lumbering town developed on its site.

PLATE 63: NOTES

JAMES ALDEN was born March 31, 1810, at Portland, Maine, a descendant of John and Priscilla Alden. He entered the United States Navy and was with Lieutenant Charles Wilkes in California in 1842, in charge of surveying and charting the Sacramento River. During the War with Mexico, Alden served with the Home Squadron at Vera Cruz. In 1848 he was assigned to the Coast Survey. From then until 1860 he was in charge of a hydrographic party engaged in surveying and charting the west coast from the Mexican boundary to Canada. When the Civil War came, Alden was placed in command of the *Richmond*. He advanced steadily in rank, being commissioned as a captain during the war, and as rear admiral in 1871. In 1872 Admiral Alden was placed in command of the European Squadron. The next year, upon retiring from the Navy, he returned to San Francisco and lived at the Palace Hotel until his death in 1877.

Admiral Alden's hobby was sketching. One of his sketchbooks is in the collection of the Washington State Historical Society. Six of his original water-color drawings, including the one reproduced here, are in the collection of the California Historical Society.

During part of the time that Alden was stationed in California he had with him a young nephew, James Madison Alden, who also was an amateur artist. As he signed his drawings "James M. Alden" they can readily be distinguished from those of the Admiral, which are signed "James Alden."

Crescent City, 1859

Artist: JAMES ALDEN

From the original water color in the California Historical Society, San Francisco.

PLATE 63

THE OPENING of mines along the lower Klamath and Smith rivers was responsible for the founding of Crescent City on the north side of a crescent-shaped bay near the Oregon border. The bay, which appears from the outside to be the mouth of a river, was first entered in 1851 by a party of treasure seekers hunting gold hidden by a legendary prospector, and was originally called Paragon Bay. At first the town flourished. A flour mill was erected, and some business in lumbering, dairying, and fishing carried on. A few people settled there after the excitement at Gold Bluffs died out and some others came there from the Klamath River mines. The little town had two hundred houses and about eight hundred people.

Although the harbor was the chief attraction, there was no pier built until 1860. Ships anchoring in the bay transferred their passengers to surf boats and then to horse-drawn carts to be hauled ashore over the shallow tidal flats. The open roadstead, which is the only pretense of a harbor north of Trinidad, and a few minor industries have kept Crescent City alive.

This sketch was made in July, 1859, when the vessels of the United States Coast Survey touched at Crescent City on their way to Washington and British Columbia.

California Cities of the 'Fifties

PLATE 64: NOTES

FRANCIS SAMUEL MARRYAT, son of Captain Frederick Marryat, the English novelist, was born in London on April 18, 1826, and entered the British navy as a midshipman at the age of fourteen. He saw duty in the Mediterranean and in the Indian Ocean. After eight years of service he returned to England, resigned his commission, and wrote his first book, *Borneo . . . with Drawings of Costume and Scenery*, which was published in 1848, the year of his father's death.

Marryat used his inheritance to outfit himself for a hunting trip to California, accompanied by a servant and three bloodhounds. He arrived in California in the late fall of '49 and while the rest of the world hunted gold he hunted deer and antelope along the Russian River.

In 1850 Marryat moved to San Francisco and while living there met his old friend, Sir Henry Huntley (author of *California, Its Gold and Its Inhabitants*, London, 1856), with whom he visited the northern mines. Marryat left for England in the spring of '52, but returned wih his wife in the fall. In the interim he wrote and published a pamphlet on quartz mining in California.

The Marryats stayed in California for a year before returning to England. In 1855 Marryat's illustrated account of his visit to California was published with the title *Mountains and Molehills*. Some of the original water colors from which the lithographs for this book were made, and a few of his unpublished paintings, have been preserved. His death at the age of twenty-nine cut short a promising career as author-artist.

San Francisco Fire, June 14, 1850

Artist: FRANCIS SAMUEL MARRYAT

From the original water color in the Society of California Pioneers, San Francisco.

PLATE 64

THE FIRST great fire in San Francisco occurred on December 24, 1849. Before volunteer bucket brigades could check the flames more than fifty houses had been consumed. On May 5, 1850, a second and greater fire burned a large portion of the business district. Rebuilding was going on at a furious rate when, on June 14, a third great fire started, destroying the district between California, Kearny, Clay, and Montgomery streets. The next fire, on September 17, burned over an area even greater than that of the May fire, but fortunately a less populous section. After each conflagration the people started rebuilding immediately, each time taking better precautions against fire hazards. The quick response of the rival volunteer fire companies, organization of which had begun on the day after the first fire, kept innumerable small fires from speading. Membership in any one of these companies was considered a great honor. The members paid for their own uniforms, paid for the furnishing of the engine houses, paid dues, even paid for their engines.

There were two more great fires in the following year, both too large for the volunteer fire companies to control, one on May 4, and the other on June 22, 1851. The May fire was the most destructive, destroying approximately $8,000,000 worth of property.

These successive fires, while disastrous to the property owners involved, had the happy result of transforming a ramshackle village of wooden shanties into a city of well-constructed homes and buildings.

PLATE 65: NOTES

ALTHOUGH the painting, "Justice Meted Out to English Jim," is unsigned, it is believed to be the work of John Prendergast, an English artist who came to San Francisco from Honolulu in July, 1848. The subject is one that he would have chosen, the painting has all the attention to detail that was characteristic of his work, and it is similar in style to paintings and lithographs which were signed by him.

Prendergast worked in crayon, pencil, and water color, and lithographs were made from some of his drawings. The best known of these is "Procession at San Francisco in Celebration of the Admission of California . . . 1850." Reproductions of four of his paintings were used to illustrate the second edition of Theodore T. Johnson's *California and Oregon* . . . (1850). A number of his unpublished drawings of San Francisco scenes have survived.

Justice Meted Out to English Jim, July 11, 1851

Artist: JOHN PRENDERGAST (?)

From the original water color. Courtesy of Mr. Roger D. Lapham.

PLATE 65

GOLD RUSH CALIFORNIA attracted a motley population. There were those who came to dig gold and those who came to rob them of it. Whole sections of San Francisco were settled by ruffians from all over the world. They roved the streets at night, robbing and murdering, totally unrestrained by San Francisco's corrupt officials. Finally a small group of reputable citizens took matters into their own hands and, on June 9, 1851, formed the first of the famous San Francisco vigilance committees.

"English Jim" was a notorious criminal from Australia, one of the infamous Sydney Ducks.

He was apprehended and brought before the committee on July 10, 1851, for some minor offense, but under questioning confessed to a whole series of atrocious crimes. The committee made short work of him. The next day, on July 11, the bell of the Monumental Fire Company tolled the customary signal for the assembling of the committee. The members, four hundred in number, formed into ranks and marched their prisoner down Battery Street to Market Street and out on the wharf where a gallows stood ready. A great crowd of spectators followed, to see English Jim pay for his crimes.

The gold rush gave additional importance to the question of a transcontinental railroad, a matter that had long been under discussion. The first step taken by Congress toward a definite plan for a railroad to the West was the authorization of a survey of possible routes. The survey was begun in 1853 and carried on until 1855, with five routes under consideration.

Charles Koppel was one of several artists engaged to delineate the topography of the country traversed. He accompanied Lieutenant Williamson, one of the officers, from New York to California by way of Panama. They arrived in San Francisco June 20, 1853, and met the rest of the members of the survey at Benicia. Koppel was assigned to that part of the work that lay in the San Joaquin, Tulare, and Los Angeles valleys.

The accomplishments of the entire undertaking fill twelve volumes of *Reports of Explorations . . .* published by the United States War Department. The drawings made by Koppel and the other artists are reproduced as lithographs or woodcuts. Koppel's view of Los Angeles, July, 1853, appears in Volume V, Part 1. Until recently it was considered the earliest view of Los Angeles, but drawings of the city made in 1849 by H. M. T. Powell have recently come to light. No other work by Koppel is known except a portrait of his friend Jefferson Davis, painted in 1865.

In 1912 Koppel's view of Los Angeles was copied in oils by Miss Petra Palanconi, a Los Angeles artist, and the painting was given to the County Museum at Los Angeles.

Los Angeles, 1853

Artist: Charles Koppel

From *Pacific Railroad Reports*, Vol. V, Part 1.

PLATE 66

T HE DISCOVERY of gold in central California had little effect upon the growth of Los Angeles, which had been founded in 1781 by Felipe de Neve, governor of California from 1775 to 1782.

Nuestra Señora la Reina de los Angeles de Porciúncula, as it was originally named, was established on the banks of the Porciúncula (now Los Angeles) River. It was the second civic pueblo established in California by the Spanish government, and by 1800 had become a thriving, though small, community. Situated in a fertile valley, several hundred miles from the gold region, it was still a small agricultural and stock-raising settlement of not more than eighty houses as late as 1853, when this view was made.

The artist sketched Los Angeles from the top of what is now known as the Broadway hill, at the site of old Fort Moore. The view is to the east-ward, looking over the valley of the San Gabriel and Los Angeles rivers. The town of Los Angeles lay at the base of a low range of hills, along the course of the rivers. The Church of the Angels stood in the center of the village, at the edge of the plaza, in a group of one-storied, flat-roofed, adobe houses. The houses formed streets but not connecting rows. They were placed at odd angles to the points of the compass so that the sunlight might be admitted to all the windows during some part of the day. The outlying districts were planted to grapes and fruits. Cattle grazed on the surrounding plains.

PLATE 67: NOTES

FESSENDEN NOTT OTIS was born in 1825, at Ballston Springs, New York. He studied art, and after becoming a successful teacher of drawing and perspective, entered medical college, from which he graduated in 1852. From 1853 until 1859 he served as a ship's surgeon for the Pacific Mail Steamship Company, in Panama and in the Pacific. He began private practice in New York in 1860 and for ten years served also as police surgeon. He was on the faculty of the College of Physicians and Surgeons and on the staff of various other medical institutions. He died at New Orleans on May 24, 1900.

In addition to numerous publications in the field of medical research, he published an *Illustrated History of the Panama Railroad* (1861). Five pictures, two of them of California subjects, are known to be his work: "San Francisco from Rincon Point," copyrighted in 1856 and reproduced here; "Foundry of the Pacific Mail Steamship Company, Benicia, California, 1855"; "View of Panama," and "The Steamship Illinois," which were drawn for Endicott's lithographs; "View of Culebra or the Summit, the Terminus of the Panama Railroad in 1854," lithographed by C. Parsons, New York.

San Francisco from Rincon Point, 1854

Artist: FESSENDEN NOTT OTIS

From a photograph of a colored lithograph. Courtesy of the Society of California Pioneers, San Francisco.

PLATE 67

By 1854 SAN FRANCISCO had become too large a city to be encompassed within one picture. The houses had climbed the slopes of Telegraph and Russian hills, had moved on out Clay Street, and semicircled around from Clark's Wharf to Rincon Point. Wharves ran out to deep water, making it possible for ships to unload their cargoes directly, instead of transferring them to lighters.

The city was lighted with gas; many miles of planked streets had been laid. Only six years had elapsed since the discovery of gold but hardly a trace remained in San Francisco of the little village of Yerba Buena. Although building had run ahead of demand, and some of the new, expensive, fireproof buildings stood tenantless, the future prosperity of San Francisco was assured.

The view reproduced here was drawn from the corner of Fremont and Harrison streets on Rincon Hill, looking north to Telegraph Hill in the background. In the middle 'fifties Rincon Hill was a fashionable residential section with ornate houses and well-cared-for gardens. The buildings in the center of the picture are standing in the area once covered by the waters of Yerba Buena Cove. The cove had gradually been filled in with sand from San Francisco's numerous and unsightly sand hills, the filled section giving the city its only level building sites. The first road clearly marked in the picture is Mission Street, the direct route out of town to the Mission Dolores. Omnibuses, handsome Brewster coaches like the one shown in the picture, ran out this street to the valley in which the Mission Dolores was situated.

PLATE 68: NOTES

"STOCKTON," a canvas measuring 37 by 70 inches, was painted by Browere in 1856, during his first visit to California. It is the only California painting by Browere that is known in which actual buildings can be identified and that is therefore important as an historical document as well as being a work of art. The vivid color of the painting, in which lies much of its charm, is characteristic of his work. Browere's large oil painting, "Columbia, 1854" (not reproduced), is the same type of painting as "Stockton." However, unlike the Stockton view, the picture has no value as a historical record, the entire scene being an artistic creation rather than a factual rendition.

For additional notes on the artist, see plates 29, 38, 44, and 50.

Stockton, 1856

Artist: ALBERTIS DEL ORIENT BROWERE

From the original oil painting in the M. H. de Young Memorial Museum, San Francisco.

PLATE 68

Although stockton probably never had the idyllic atmosphere that the artist has given it, the frequent fires which ravaged it in the early years of its existence had done much to clean up its unsightly districts and bring its appearance to an approximation of that in the picture.

From the first days of the gold discovery Stockton shared importance with Sacramento as a supply depot for the mines. It was strategically situated on the San Joaquin River so that both river and road traffic to the southern mines passed through it. Many petty criminals were attracted to this new trade center and for many years Stockton was widely known as a tough, lawbreaking town.

The view looks toward the head of Stockton Channel and the center of town. On the left, just beyond the sailboat, is the entrance to McLeod's Lake. Weber Point is in the middle distance. Captain Charles Weber's house is the white one with the cupola. To the left of Captain Weber's house can be seen the canted masts of the U. S. Brig *Adelaide*, which lay at anchor in McLeod's Lake for fifteen years. The houses on the right-hand side stand between Stockton Channel and Mormon Channel. Those on the far right are on the outskirts of South Stockton. The large modern-looking buildings, many of brick, standing throughout the town, were erected after the fires of the early 'fifties had wiped out the original canvas and wooden shanties of the business district. There was almost as great a difference between the Stockton of 1856 and that of 1849 (plate 37) as there is between the town depicted here and the thriving inland port of today.

PLATE 69: NOTES

"SACRAMENTO, 1857" was drawn by Baker in the spring of '57. Subscriptions were solicited for lithographic copies, to cost $5.00 each. The little red book now in the collection of the Society of California Pioneers, in which Baker kept a list of the subscribers, gives the artist's announcement of the picture:

To the Public:—The subscriber respectfully solicits the patronage of the public to a work of art which must appeal somewhat to the patriotism and public spirit of every citizen who rejoices in the good name of Sacramento. The beautiful "City of the Plain" has often been represented but on account of the level nature of its site no one comprehensive view has ever been taken from actual observation. The work which now claims your attention is the result of some months labor and is calculated to fill this void. It exhibits at a glance the situation and appearance of Sacramento as seen from the height of the ordinary flight of a bird, and is thus intended to be published as a bird's eye view of Sacramento ... If subscription warrants there will be published a small handbook to accompany the picture.

Enough subscriptions were obtained to make possible two editions of a lithographic copy of the drawing. The reproduction shown here was made from the original drawing.

For additional notes on the artist, see plate 36.

Sacramento, 1857

Artist: GEORGE HOLBROOK BAKER

From the original pencil drawing in the M. H. de Young Memorial Museum, San Francisco.

PLATE 69

DURING THE gold rush years Sacramento profited immensely from the mining trade. The town, which in 1848 consisted of a few houses on Front Street between J and K streets, had by 1857 been built up almost solidly from I to R streets and from Front to Twelfth streets. The city became the state capital in 1854.

The picture reproduced here was one of the ever-popular "bird's eye" views. At the left-hand margin of the picture is I Street, bordering Sutter Lake (first called China Slough). The Sacramento River, paralleled by Front Street, forms the lower margin of the picture. The building occupied by the state offices was on I Street between Sixth and Seventh streets, near the east end of Sutter Lake. On the embarcadero, at the foot of J Street, was the *La Grange*, Sacramento's floating jail. From the J Street landing a water taxi ran to Suttersville. Further along the embarcadero, to the right, were the shipping offices of the river lines. The large building on Front Street between L and M streets was intended by one of Sacramento's ambitious citizens to be the state capitol. It was used for some of the county offices. On the water front between O and P streets was a curious floating fish market, a bargelike craft surrounded by half-submerged crates of lobsters, shrimps, salmon, etc. The train coming into town along R Street was one of those owned by the Sacramento Valley Railroad. The line was twenty-two and a half miles long, connected Sacramento and Folsom, and was the first railroad in the State of California.

INDEX OF ARTISTS